Ethnobotany

The Green World

Ethnobotany

Kim J. Young

Series Editor
William G. Hopkins
Professor Emeritus of Biology
University of Western Ontario

CHELSEA HOUSE
PUBLISHERS
An imprint of Infobase Publishing

Ethnobotany
Copyright © 2007 by Infobase Publishing

Chelsea House
An imprint of Infobase Publishing
132 West 31st Street
New York NY 10001

Library of Congress Cataloging-in-Publication Data

Young, Kim J.
  Ethnobotany / Kim J. Young.
      p. cm. — (The green world)
  Includes bibliographical references and index.
  ISBN 0-7910-8963-0
  1. Ethnobotany—Juvenile literature. 2. Human-plant relationships—Juvenile literature.
I. Title. II. Series.
  GN476.73.Y68 2006
  581.6'3—dc22   2006011018

Chelsea House books are available at special discounts when purchased in bulk quantities for businesses, associations, institutions, or sales promotions. Please call our Special Sales Department in New York at (212) 967-8800 or (800) 322-8755.

You can find Chelsea House on the World Wide Web at http://www.chelseahouse.com

Text design by Keith Trego
Cover design by Ben Peterson
Composition by Hermitage Publishing Services
Cover printed by IBT Global, Troy, NY
Book printed and bound by IBT Global, Troy, NY
Date printed: November 2009
Printed in the United States of America

10 9 8 7 6 5 4 3 2

This book is printed on acid-free paper.

All links, web addresses and Internet search terms were checked and verified to be correct at the time of publication. Because of the dynamic nature of the web, some addresses and links may have changed since publication and may no longer be valid.

Table of Contents

Introduction

By William G. Hopkins

"Have you thanked a green plant today?" reads a popular bumper sticker. Indeed we should thank green plants for providing the food we eat, fiber for the clothing we wear, wood for building our houses, and the oxygen we breathe. Without plants, humans and other animals simply could not exist. Psychologists tell us that plants also provide a sense of well-being and peace of mind, which is why we preserve forested parks in our cities, surround our homes with gardens, and install plants and flowers in our homes and workplaces. Gifts of flowers are the most popular way to acknowledge weddings, funerals, and other events of passage. Gardening is one of the fastest growing hobbies in North America and the production of ornamental plants contributes billions of dollars annually to the economy.

Human history has been strongly influenced by plants. The rise of agriculture in the Fertile Crescent of Mesopotamia brought previously scattered hunter-gatherers together into villages. Ever since, the availability of land and water for cultivating plants has been a major factor in determining the location of human settlements. World exploration and discovery was driven by the search for herbs and spices. The cultivation of New World crops—sugar, cotton, and tobacco—was responsible for the introduction of slavery to America, the human and social consequences of which are still with us. The push westward by English colonists into the rich lands of the Ohio River valley in the mid-1700s was driven by the need to increase corn production and was a factor in precipitating the French and Indian War. The Irish potato famine in 1847 set in motion a wave of migration, mostly to North America, that would reduce the population of Ireland by half over the next 50 years.

As a young university instructor directing biology tutorials in a classroom that looked out over a wooded area, I would ask each group of students to look out the window and tell me what they saw. More often than not the question would be met with a blank, questioning look. Plants are so much a part of our environment and the fabric of our everyday lives that they rarely register in our conscious thought. Yet today, faced with disappearing rain forests, exploding population growth, urban sprawl, and concerns about climate change, the productive capacity of global agricultural and forestry ecosystems is put under increasing pressure. Understanding plants is even more essential as we attempt to build a sustainable environment for the future.

The Green World series opens doors to the world of plants. The series describes what plants are, what plants do, and where plants fit into the overall scheme of things. In *Ethnobotany*, we learn of the central importance of plants to both ancient and modern cultures and especially the links between the use of plants in religious ceremonies, traditional healing remedies, and modern medicine.

1 What Is Ethnobotany?

When one tugs at a single thing in nature,
he finds it attached to the rest of the world.

—John Muir (1838–1919)
American environmentalist, naturalist, explorer, and writer

What Is Ethnobotany?

Google the word *ethnobotany* from your computer. Approximately 3,000 listings featuring a variety of descriptions about how plants were used in primitive cultures will appear on your screen. Within the definitions will be words like *indigenous, rain forest, ancient, pharmaceuticals, folklore, hallucinogens,* and *endangered.* However, if you try to look up *ethnobotany* in the latest edition of *Webster's New World College Dictionary* you will not find an entry.

Ask an archeologist to explain ethnobotany and you may receive a scholarly lecture on hawthorne seeds found among the bones of a Delaware Indian ossuary. Ask a chemist to describe ethnobotany and you may learn about the pharmaceutical benefits of *Digitalis* (also called foxglove) as a treatment for heart disease. Visit a Navajo sweat lodge and experience ethnobotany yourself when a brew of water, cedar, and pinon needles is poured over searing red rocks to release spiritual and physical healing vapors.

So, what is ethnobotany? It is all of these things. Ethnobotany is a subject that fills volumes of historical and biological texts yet is a subject largely ignored in modern language texts. It is an ancient way of life and a relatively new and thriving scientific field.

Perhaps the simplest definition of ethnobotany is provided by the word itself: *ethno* (people) and *botany* (science of plants). In essence, it is a study of how people of particular cultures and regions make use of the plants in their local environments. These uses can include as food, medicine, fuel, shelter, and in many cultures, in religious ceremonies.

WHAT DOES AN ETHNOBOTANIST DO?

In 1895, during a lecture in Philadelphia, a botanist named John Harshberger used the term *ethnobotany* to describe his work. He described his research as the study of "plants used by primitive and aboriginal people." At first, ethnobotany meant simply listing plants and some of their uses. Many scientists did not consider the indigenous people who used those plants to be important. Harshberger provided the first definition of *ethnobotany* as the study of *how* native tribes used plants for food, shelter, or clothing.[1]

As ethnobotany evolved, it became clear that ethnobotanists must understand not only the complex relationships people held with plants, but also how the plants themselves interacted with other plants, as perceived by those people who knew them best.

Practical techniques for the ethnobotanist in the field began to take shape as Harshberger and others who followed in his footsteps created a template for study in the field (Figure 1.1). In their research, ethnobotanists need to be prepared to ask the following questions:

- What are the fundamental ideas and conceptions of people living in a particular region about the plant life surrounding them?

- What effect does a given environment have on the lives, customs, religion, thoughts, and everyday practical affairs of the people studied?

- In what ways do the people make use of the local plants for food, medicine, material culture, and ceremonial purposes?

- How much knowledge do the people have of the parts, functions, and activities of plants?

- How are plant names categorized in the language of the people studied, and what can the study of these names reveal about the culture of the people?

One of the best-known modern ethnobotanists was Richard Evans Schultes. An important voice for the cultures and regional environments where his research work was carried out, Schultes identified the field of ethnobotany as an interdisciplinary field, combining botany, anthropology, economics, ethics, history, chemistry, and many other areas of study.

Figure 1.1 An ethnobotanist with the International Plant Genetic Resources Institute in Cali, Colombia, receives a local strain of peanut from a native farmer in the Amazonian lowlands of Ecuador.

Ethnobotanists help clarify the important difference between how and in what ways people *use* nature, and how and in what ways people *perceive* nature. It is an important distinction. When ethnobotanists gather data from a group of people, they are searching for clues on how these people's ancestors used plants for food, medicine, construction materials, and tools. Ethnobotanists take this research a step further to reveal how people *perceive* their place within the environment.

Today we are alienated from our environment. We think of the environment as a place to visit, to hike through, or to bird-watch. In contrast, consider that some indigenous people do not even have a word in their language to describe their own native ecosystems. Instead they regard the environment as an extension of themselves and literally are unable to separate the environment from their own self.

A goal of modern civilization is to insulate people from the environment. We try to control the weather with air-conditioning and home heating. We destroy natural habitats in order to build a home or office, then sparsely relandscape with plants that are not native to the region (Figure 1.2). As we continue to alienate ourselves from the natural world, it may be that one of ethnobotany's greatest contributions will be to close the gap between nature and man.

NEW WORD, OLD IDEA

The use of plants by people is not new. Plant life has existed on Earth for hundreds of millions of years—longer than humans

Figure 1.2 A newly constructed highway cuts through dense forest in British Columbia, Canada. Development, such as this highway, has significantly altered the way that humans interact with nature.

have been around. Most scientists believe that plants made Earth's atmosphere livable for humans and animals by changing carbon dioxide into the oxygen that we all breathe. Today, plants are still responsible for our survival.

Despite this historical relationship, you will likely not see the term *ethnobotany* used in any historical text. You will, however, find descriptions of plant-collecting field trips and detailed descriptions of plants and their uses dating to pre-classical times. The earliest documented uses of plants for medicinal purposes were found in Babylon circa 1770 B.C. in the **Code of Hammurabi** and in ancient Egypt circa 1550 B.C. Plants found within the Giza pyramids proved that ancient Egyptians believed that medicinal plants had a role in the spiritual afterlife of their **pharaohs.**

Arab armies, in times of war, routinely returned from their conquests with many new plants. The Romans, on their crusades across Europe, sought local herbalists to help their troops. In the Old World, plants were often regarded as currency: Ancient trade routes established for the sales of exotic spices and plants have been documented.

Spanish **conquistadors** kept records of the plants used by the native peoples they encountered when they arrived in the Americas. Christopher Columbus was actually in search of cash crops like pepper and nutmeg when he landed on American soil (Figure 1.3).

Nomadic people sharing and exchanging their local botanical recipes, cures, and potions with neighboring tribes during their travels preserved important new information about plants. Passed from generation to generation, this knowledge became evidence that plants had been studied and used to improve lives since very early in recorded human history.

INDIGENOUS KNOWLEDGE

Indigenous, or native, people have always had a significant relationship with the ecosystems in which they live. These ecosys-

Figure 1.3 Christopher Columbus is depicted arriving on the shores of the New World in 1492. Columbus was actually trying to reach Asia, where he hoped to find exotic plants and spices to bring back to Europe.

tems are vital for their survival, providing a wide array of plants for food, shelter, and tools. Those plants also provide sources for the medicines and religious rituals that are woven into the native cultures. As the ecosystems provide a kind of revenue for indigenous people, they, in turn, serve as stewards of their environments and have done so for generations.

What is indigenous knowledge? It is the awareness and ability of native people to create practical and lifesaving products from their environments. It refers to the close interrelationship between the environment and aspects of their culture. Indigenous knowledge is an oral tradition that is shared within a native person's own culture.

The Ethnobotanist in the Field

Ethnobotanists are required to spend part of their time in front of a computer, in an office, or in a laboratory. But staying indoors would make it impossible for the scientist to perform his or her main duties—identifying and collecting plants, and interviewing the people living closest to those plants.

So what is the ethnobotanist's job like? Imagine a job where warm sandy beaches massage your feet or dark brackish muck oozes between your toes. Picture yourself in the tropical waters of Costa Rica, or maneuvering through decomposing vegetation of the humid Brazilian rain forest. Listen to the siren-like calls of lemurs and follow leaf-tailed geckos as you trek through Madagascar. You will know the sensation of insects crawling over your skin while you taste native dishes and your clothes absorb the smoke of ceremonial fires. This is the life of an ethnobotanist.

Ethnobotanists, like explorers walking across the Sahara or naturalists paddling the Amazon, still travel the mostly hidden corners of the world. And like those who came before them, they still collect plants, preserving them for the laboratory by pressing them between sheets of newspapers or storing them in alcohol. Natural history notes, artistic sketches, compass orientations, and current weather conditions are all recorded in journals while riding canoes downstream or navigating a dense jungle.

Technology plays a part, too. Satellite images identify clusters of vegetation from above, giving the ethnobotanist access to larger landscapes. Digital photography allows the field researcher to forward photographs of live plants directly to botanists in other parts of the world for assistance in the identification of a particular species. Answers arrive within hours or days, rather than the typical months or years for dried specimens that had to be hiked out and shipped over sea to foreign continents in the past. Computers provide information and communication almost immediately. Perhaps technology removes some of the romance of the idea of field research, but at a time when our ecosystems are disappearing at an alarming rate, technology is as welcome an aid as mosquito netting, a compass, and fire.

Indigenous knowledge is both sacred and secular. Items from the environment are used for ceremonies and rituals and for artistic creations such as song, dance, and storytelling. Indigenous knowledge of ecosystems incorporates important methods of hunting, fishing, and gathering in order to secure these natural resources and provide for the survival of the people.

FOLKLORE VS. SCIENCE

Some people consider indigenous knowledge to be merely folklore and not based on scientific facts. However, folklore should not be dismissed or confused with a child's fairy tale. Folklore should be understood as part of the history of a culture, as passed down from generation to generation. Ethnobotanists are highly interested in folklore—the anecdotes, mythologies, rituals, and communications with plants and their spirits—and understand that regional folklore provides the keys to the character and meaning a plant has to local cultures.

Traditional healers of all cultures follow the folklore approach to learning about plant use. Traditional healers are the people who can, without the use of advanced scientific equipment or formal schooling, identify plants, decide their uses, and discover their curative powers. It is of great interest to the ethnobotanist to discover how the traditional healer learns to combine several plant species to achieve greater remedy effectiveness, and also how the healer controls potentially dangerous doses.

Understanding plant lore requires studying the value systems of the people who tell the stories. The ethnobotanist performing field research today understands that to fully understand and appreciate native plants, he or she must be knowledgeable both in the study of plants and in the observation of the indigenous culture.

2 The Classification of Plants

What's in a name? That which we call a
rose by any other word would smell as sweet.
—William Shakespeare (1564–1616)
English poet and playwright

The Classification of Plants

Ethnobotany raises many questions. Perhaps the question most often asked is why plants have traditionally been the focus of so much research. Why not study the relationships between various cultures and the wildlife they live among? In his book, *Plants, People, and Culture*, Michael J. Balick provides a succinct answer: "Plants produce, while animals consume."

Plants are considered producers because they *produce* their own food. With few exceptions, animals (including human beings) survive by consuming something else. Green plants are among the only organisms on Earth that can take energy from the sun, absorb water and nutrients from the soil, and take carbon dioxide from the atmosphere to create their own food. Thus, green plants begin the food chain.

The leaves of green plants contain a special green pigment called chlorophyll. When light strikes a plant's leaves, chlorophyll transforms carbon dioxide and water into a sugar called glucose. The sugar is then transported through tubes in the leaf to the plant's roots, stems, and fruits. The extra oxygen left over from the water is released back into the air. This entire process is called **photosynthesis**. Almost every living creature on Earth depends on photosynthesis (Figure 2.1).

In addition to creating food, most plants are bound by their biological and physical design to remain standing and rooted in the soil. This stationary position combined with an enormous production of cellulose—the main portion of plant tissue—make plants the most stable and reliable source of food and building materials known to man. Animals do not provide for us in quite the same way. We harvest animals to use for food, and we also use their bones, hides, and furs—but harvesting animals involves more work, and presumably more danger. Fortunately for us, plants generally do not try to elude capture or turn to attack whomever or whatever is harvesting them or eating them.

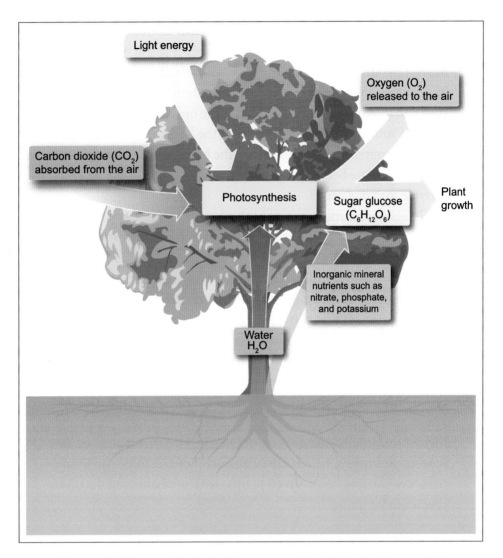

Figure 2.1 Photosynthesis is the process in which plants use light energy to make sugar out of carbon dioxide and water. As a result of photosynthesis, plants release oxygen into the air.

That may seem like an absurd point, but imagine a world where your food does not appear on the shelves of the grocery store in neatly wrapped cellophane packages, tin cans, or cardboard boxes. What if you were expected to hunt your own food each morning for that day's school lunch? Your fondness for cheeseburgers might diminish considerably if you actually had to harvest the cow and process the meat yourself. Or suppose you are in search of a new leather coat but your choice of animal tries to turn you into its own dinner? What if the only materials available to build your small shelter came from the bones and tanned hide of a wild animal? You may suffer at the hands of the elements for quite some time before you finally track down and kill a beast to provide for your needs.

Plants are far more accessible and safer to harvest. Although some cultures rely on meat for sustenance, most cultures rely on plants for the bulk of their diets. There *are* cultures that rarely eat plants, like the tundra Inuit or African Kalahari tribesmen, but even they must rely on plants to provide forage for the wild animals they hunt or the domestic herds they shepherd across the landscape (Figure 2.2).

Simply put, plants are necessary for the continuation of life on Earth. They are an integral part of the food chain, supplying energy and oxygen for the higher, more complex life forms. Plants are found everywhere on Earth except the polar zones, the highest mountains, the deepest oceans, and the driest parts of the deserts. According to scientists, almost 90 percent of the living mass on Earth is made up of plants, with an estimated 400,000 species to be found.[2]

THE NUTRIENT CYCLE WITHIN PLANTS

The defining chemical unit among living things is the carbon molecule. Carbon atoms originate from the carbon dioxide found in the atmosphere. The atoms enter the living world through the process of photosynthesis in green plants, algae, and some kinds of bacteria. Known as primary producers, the green plants, algae, and bacteria originate the cycle of consumption, decay, and respiration that incorporates carbon into more complex organic compounds, which are subsequently broken down to create energy.

Figure 2.2 Two Inuits wearing hooded full-length fur parkas bend over to pick berries in Alaska in this photograph from 1929. Although plant life can be scarce in Alaska, plants are still a valuable part of the Inuit diet.

Photosynthesis is the process by which green leaves make energy in the form of carbohydrates. In addition to recombining carbon atoms from carbon dioxide into sugars used as food for the plant, the sugars produced by photosynthesis are also linked to create polymers such as starch and cellulose. It is this cellulose, when combined with plant resins, that forms one of the most important building materials we have: wood.

As plants compete with one another for the sun, it is their particular location in an ecosystem and their position within the plant **canopy** that enables each plant to capture the light that powers the photosynthetic process. Competition for sunlight explains why all plants grow in an upward direction. Their leaves must be exposed to sunlight. Large woody trees like oaks and sycamores have strong trunks to support their weight as they grow skyward. Poison ivy (*Toxicodendron radicans*) and Virginia creeper vines (*Parthenocissus quinquefolia*) depend on strong trees to provide them with a stable frame on which to grow toward the sun. Smaller shrubs and forest understory species such as spicebush (*Lindera benzoin*) and highbush blueberry (*Vaccinium corymbosum*) have distinct leaf patterns ensuring that no leaf lies in the shade of another leaf. The same competition explains why leaves are paper-thin, thus increasing the opportunity for light to pass through both sides.

Virtually all life on Earth depends on, and competes for, the sun's energy. But only green plants are able to convert this energy, through photosynthesis, into a chemical energy that they can use. When this energy is stored in the form of simple sugars, green plants become producers. As creatures consume plants, that energy begins to cycle throughout the environment.

BOTANY IS THE STUDY OF PLANTS

Botany is a science divided into many areas. Plant **taxonomy** describes plants and arranges them into groups. Plant geography is concerned with the location of certain plants. Plant ecology examines the relationship between plants and their environment. Paleobotany focuses on ancient plants, phytopathology on plant disease, and economic botany on how plants can be used in commercial products. Plant morphology refers to the physical structure of plants, including the function of the plant parts (physiology), the study of plant cells (cytology), and the anatomy and histology, or internal structure, of the plants. And, of course, there is ethnobotany, the study of the relationship between plants and cultures.

Regardless of the specific field of botany on which he or she is focused, no botanist can move forward with research without some understanding of plant classification. Plant classification helps keep track of our planet's vast biodiversity and helps us understand the ecological systems that support that biodiversity. Botanists are constantly exploring how the genetic diversity of plants and their sensitivity to particular environments might provide solutions to such problems as overpopulation and disease. Plant classification plays a large role in ethnobotanical research.

HOW ARE PLANTS CLASSIFIED?

Taxonomy is the process of classifying living organisms into categories. For the ethnobotanist, understanding how plants are classified enables him or her to better understand local and specialized plants, the physical properties of the plants, and the similarities and differences between different types of plants.

Science classifies plants into an orderly system through which they can be readily identified. In the five-kingdom classification system found in most biological texts, plants share certain characteristics. First, they are multicellular and eukaryotic—meaning that there is a membrane surrounding the nucleus of each of their cells. The light-absorbing molecules of plants include chlorophyll and carotenoid pigments. Finally, plants have the ability to store food in the form of starch and have cell walls that are made mostly of cellulose.

In addition to plants, the other organisms categorized in the five-kingdom classification system are animals, monera (which includes bacteria), protista (single-celled organisms), and fungi (once considered plants, but now classified in a kingdom of their own).

The plant world can be further broken down into the bryophytes (mosses and liverworts), the pteridophytes (ferns, horsetails, and club mosses), the gymnosperms (conifers, yews, cycads, and ginkgos), and the angiosperms (flowering plants).

Three of the above, the pteridophytes, the gymnosperms, and the angiosperms, are also classified as **vascular** plants (Figure 2.3). Vascular refers to an internal transport system that allows certain plants to be less dependent on water in the surrounding environment.

Of these groups, the pteridophytes, or ferns, are the most primitive—dominating ancient Earth before the other two groups appeared. Eventually, however, the environment favored the gymnosperms and angiosperms that now dominate plant life.

The classification continues to narrow with the gymnosperms and angiosperms, which are collectively known as the seed plants.

Figure 2.3 The Virginia pine, *Pinus virginiana*, is both a gymnosperm and a vascular plant.

Of these two groups, the angiosperms, or flowering plants, are the most advanced of the groups. Most land plants familiar to us belong to this group, which includes plants of every shape and size from grasses to cactuses, tiny herbs to wildflowers, and dogwoods to large oaks. This huge and diverse group is divided again into two subgroups, the **monocotyledons** and the **dicotyledons.**

The monocotyledons include grasses, lilies, and palm trees; the dicotyledons are trees such as maples and oaks, and flowers such as dandelions, goldenrod, and buttercups.

WHY DO WE CLASSIFY PLANTS?

We classify plants to avoid confusion. We know plants by their common names, many of which we learned as children. For example, buttercups (*Ranuculus*) are soft yellow flowers found in early spring meadows. If you like gardening, your grandparents or parents might have taught you that African marigolds (*Taretes erecta*) provide a splash of color and a little pest control for carrots and squash. You may be familiar with the tulip poplars (*Liriodendron tulipera*), dogwoods (*Cornus*), and eastern white pines (*Pinus strobus*) that shelter our homes and shade our schoolyards. But simply referring to the common name of a plant is often confusing. One plant can have many different common names. The red maple is common to Pennsylvania and the swamp maple is common in Connecticut. As it turns out, they are the same plant (*Acer rubrum*), but with at least two colloquial names (and undoubtedly more). Similarly confusing: African marigolds are not native to Africa, but to Mexico instead.

There is a white lily in Europe that is believed to have at least 245 different common names, and the marsh marigold has as many as 280. Clearly, knowing *only* the common name of a plant is not an accurate method of understanding or identifying a particular plant.

For this reason, botanists use a more precise way of naming, known as classification or taxonomy. Scientific classification helps us not only by naming organisms, but also by providing a key to understanding how a plant functions. Scientists name plants to give them a unique placing in their ecosystem and to explain their relationships with other organisms in that ecosystem.

Plant classification can be complicated. Plant species can resemble one another quite closely; plants can sometimes inter-breed within species or across species, producing hybrids and varieties that sometimes defy classification. The *Cinchona* tree is distinguished by its bark, which possesses an **alkaloid** derivative called **quinine**. An important plant for treating malaria outbreaks, the tree has so many species and hybrids and varieties within each species that it is almost impossible to classify. Botanists do not know the exact number of species of cinchona trees that actually exist. Even worse, "cinchona" is also a common name used to describe many different medicinal plants, further com-plicating this plant's classification.

THE BINOMIAL SYSTEM OF CLASSIFICATION

Plants are classified in several different ways. The scientific, or botanical, name given to a plant helps define its place in the bio-logical world. The binomial system of classification was created by eighteenth-century Swedish botanist Carolus Linnaeus. Lin-naeus gave each plant a scientific name with two parts: the **genus** and **species**. The genus and species are always italicized, written in Latin, and the genus is always capitalized.

The genus, or generic name, of a plant is a noun that usually names some aspect of a plant. For example the coffee plant is classified as *Coffea arabica*. *Coffea* is Latin for *kahwah*, the Arabic word for "beverage."

The species, or specific name, is usually an adjective that describes the genus. In the case of coffee, the species is *arabica*, indicating that the plant was thought to originate in Arabia. The coffee plant's botanical name, *Coffea arabica*, is therefore unique to that particular plant the world over.

Botanical names might be followed by a letter or letters that stand for the botanist who named that plant. The coffee plant's complete botanical name is *Coffea arabica L.,* with the "L" standing for Linnaeus.

Linnaeus's landmark book *Species Plantarum* ("The Species of Plants"), published in the mid-eighteenth century, continues to influence the naming of plants today. When a botanist needs to know whether a name has been used previously, this is where he or she begins. If a question arises, the earliest name for a plant is usually the official name.

WHAT THE NAMES MEAN

In addition to identifying a plant, the genus and species often tell us something about the plant. They can describe the appearance of the plant, reflect the common name of the plant, indicate a chemical in the plant, tell how the plant tastes or smells, or describe how the plant grows. The genus or species name can honor someone, such as the person who discovered the plant, or the country where the plant was first identified. An example is *Erythroxylum coca.* The genus is named after *erythro-* meaning "red" and *xylo-* meaning "wood." The species name, *coca,* is also the common name of the plant. The jaborandi tree (*Pilocarpus jaborandi*) has a genus name reflecting that the alkaloid pilocarpine can be extracted from the plant. *Jaborandi* means "one who makes saliva or one who spits," referring to the use of the plant as an expectorant (a substance that helps to clear mucus from the respiratory tract).[3] The proper classification of these plants helps the ethnobotanist identify the functional properties and relationships of plants within ecosystems.

3 The Emergence of Agriculture

*Those who labour in the earth are the chosen
people of God, if ever he had a chosen people.*

—Thomas Jefferson (1743–1826)
Third president of the United States

The Emergence of Agriculture

In the early 1990s, the Smithsonian Institute's Museum of Natural History in Washington, D.C., opened an impressive new exhibit called Seeds of Change, A Quincentennial Commemoration. The exhibition explored the consequences of the Old and New Worlds coming into contact with one another as a result of Christopher Columbus discovering America. The debate about whether Columbus actually discovered America was not part of the exhibit. Instead, the famous museum challenged visitors to understand the impact one part of the world had on another.

The arrival of Europeans on American soil affected the course of history in many significant ways—disease, warfare, and slavery among them. Amidst the tragedy, however, there were positive interactions as well. This time in history was marked by the exchange of plants across the globe, a development that changed life for many cultures. In some cases, it only took one plant to change a culture. According to Seeds of Change, the introduction of the South American potato provided Europe with an easily stored food that, along with improved health care, supported a major increase in that part of the world's human population. The importation of corn to Africa from the New World helped create a healthier, larger population there, as well.

The world was never the same once food was exchanged between cultures. As new foods fed growing populations, the industry of agriculture grew to meet those needs. Farming became a necessity for the production of food in large quantities, but agriculture on that scale came at a cost. The large **monocultures** created by this growing industry had a downside: relying on only one crop can spell disaster, as we know from Ireland's great potato famine in the mid-nineteenth century. Originally native to Peru, where it was a staple in the diet of the Incas, the potato eventually found its way to Europe by way of Spanish explorers at the end of the sixteenth century. By the mid-sixteenth century, the potato was growing in the lush soils of Ireland as an entire population began to establish a new form of farming dependent upon the New World crop and little else. When a fungus arrived from America, the potato crop was destroyed. As many as one million people died as a consequence of the resulting famine (Figure 3.1). Hundreds of thousands more immigrated across the Atlantic to America. The Emerald Isle learned a hard lesson during the great potato famine. Whether in a crop field or a natural ecosystem, diversity creates stability. Diversity is healthy

Figure 3.1 The Irish potato famine had a devastating effect on Irish society in the mid-nineteenth century. In this illustration, hungry peasants seize the crop of an evicted tenant in Kerry, Ireland.

for any ecosystem, and relying on only one crop or one or two natural plants always poses a risk.

One of the many advantages of agriculture was that for the first time in history human beings lived permanently in one place. This was new to populations that had previously been known mostly as hunters and gatherers. It is not an exaggeration to state that the sudden change from hunting wild game and harvesting seasonal wild crops to time spent gaining one's living from a single piece of ground wholly altered mankind. Agriculture also had drastic effects on the environment.

To pursue agriculture is essentially to live in one spot and exploit a relatively small piece of land intensively and over a long period of time. For approximately 10,000 years, farming around the world has evolved and assumed many forms, depending on the plants and animals available locally. Gradually, this sedentary way of life became the dominant mode of life in nearly all of the areas of the world inhabited by humans.

The earliest agricultural sites in the world were found in the Nile valley and western Asia, in the valleys of Iran's Zagros Mountains, in what is now called Turkey, in northern Syria, and along the Jordan River valley.[4] Eventually other regions around the world developed similar agricultural techniques and evolved similar cultural adaptations. These regions included the north China plains, south and southeast Asia, sub-Saharan Africa, and North and South America. Once agricultural civilizations were established, human populations started to grow, and this growth was accompanied by a demand for more food.

This new way of life and sudden dependence on relatively few plants—the main crops that humans now grew—rather than on the many different kinds of wild plants that hunter-gatherers collected created fresh concerns. The dependence on fewer plants led to greater vulnerability from weather conditions, insect infestations, and outbreaks of fungal or bacterial diseases. Betting your family's future on weather conditions that may or may not favor the growth of the particular crops you planted could be dangerous. Weather patterns fluctuate and rainfall tends to be unpredictable. In contrast, the hunter-gatherers collected food from perhaps a hundred different plant species. Some of those plants flourished in wet weather, some in dry, some were cold-resistant, and some tolerated drought. With the emergence of agriculture,

Seed-Saving

Once societies became agricultural, people learned to wisely practice seed-saving. To ensure food for the coming seasons, some crops would have been allowed to plants a seed, instead of being harvested. The seeds from the best plants would be collected, stored, and saved for planting the following year, thereby providing some security against whatever natural or man-made disasters might threaten their future.

Seed-saving has now become an urgent conservation method for preserving the historic and endangered genetic strains of old or heirloom plants. Many of the seed varieties now available through heirloom organizations have been passed down for generations from family member to family member.

One such historic plant seed is available from an organization called the Seed Savers Exchange in Decorah, Iowa. In their catalog they offer a variety of bean called The Cherokee Trail of Tears bean. The late Dr. John Wyche gave the original beans to the organization. According to his family history, Dr. Wyche's Cherokee ancestors carried this variety of bean over the infamous Trail of Tears. Beginning in October of 1838 in the Smokey Mountains and eventually ending on March 26, 1839, in the Indian Territory now known as Oklahoma, the Cherokee death march left behind a trail of over 4,000 graves.

Many seed-saving organizations offer varieties of seeds with similar fascinating and important histories that demonstrate the relationship between people and plants.

mankind started to leave behind a way of life that ensured that some sources of food were always available no matter the weather or time of year.

In the beginning, farming risked the lives of the villagers on the frailties of weather and the hardiness of the few varieties of plants cultivated but reduced the risks and challenges of rough and constant travel and encouraged population growth. For our ancestors, farming continued their dependence on natural ecological systems, but it raised the odds of disaster in any given year since farming was still more vulnerable to changes in the weather than hunting and gathering had ever been.

Farming created other challenges as well. For the first time in history humans were dependent on just a few harvests each year for the entire year's food supply. Hunter-gatherers knew how to find game and seed, nuts and berries no matter the season. Agriculturists now needed to gather all their food for the year in a few harvests, rather than gathering year round. This placed high importance on the narrow window of opportunity for planting, cultivating, and the time-consuming harvest. There were additional pressures, not least of which was how to properly store their harvest so as to provide food for the rest of the year. The food now needed to be protected from moisture (which could lead to life-threatening molds), from ingenious and often dangerous wildlife (in search of their own food), and from other people.

Fights and arguments about equal shares would no doubt accompany some harvests, as new food supplies would be handed out to members of a village in measured amounts. There were new pressures to ensure survival that required the selection, harvesting, and preservation of this year's seeds for next year's plantings. One could no longer depend on wild crops to naturally spread their own seeds throughout the environment via the wind, water, or an animal's digestive system. When you farm, you are responsible for the collection, storage, and dispersal of the seeds that will feed you in the future. Some of your crop must be saved to allow it to produce seeds, so even when hungry the first farmers learned that some food could not be eaten.

Agriculture forced people to plan for the future, instead of consuming whatever was available at the moment. The farmer who tried to live as the hunter-gatherers did would soon starve.

Hunter-gatherer groups suffered high mortality rates, especially among the young and elderly. Their way of life simply did not permit large families. New farming civilizations did not face the same pressures from natural food limits, predators, and inhospitable terrain. In contrast, as farming grew, large families

The Celebrations of Harvest

The Thanksgiving holiday in the United States is not the only example of people celebrating a successful farming season. Festivals in honor of the year's harvest are found throughout the world. In Egypt, some ancient tombs feature paintings that demonstrate the value of grains and farming from the earliest civilizations. Farmed grains fed growing populations, helped establish new communities, and likely led to the formation of new social hierarchies and governments. It is no wonder that the plants that sustained our very existence were worshipped and viewed as symbols of the power of life.

In the African countries of Ghana and Nigeria, yams are offered to the gods and to the ancestors of the villagers before the popular crops are shared with the rest of the village. Ireland celebrates the grains that make its breads, ales, and mead during the Lughnasadh, or Lammas, festival. The autumn ritual marks the time of year when people ended a period of dependence on the previous year's grain and begin to eat the current year's harvest. In Malaysia, the harvest festival honors the rice gods with fairs, farm shows, buffalo races, and wine. Entire communities harvest rice stalks with special knives believed to appeal to the rice spirit, Semangat. For the Malaysians, rice is life.

with many children meant more hands to help in the fields. As agriculture overtook the hunter-gather lifestyle, human populations began to increase and continued to build. After 10,000 years of this way of life, the human population is still expanding. Today, there are more than six billion people living on Earth and almost all of them are supported by agriculture.

Agriculture has led to more threats to our health, too. Infectious disease is a problem closely related to population growth because of the difficulty of maintaining clean, healthy living spaces in crowded conditions. Humans share many diseases with domestic animals, so clustering humans and animals together in unsanitary villages created a perfect environment for pathogens of all kinds. As a result, early village life provided a breeding ground for new and deadly diseases. It was inevitable that in these conditions, previously rare epidemics became common and serious threats to people.

In addition to inviting disease, the progress of intensive farming resulted in the destruction of forests as more land was cleared to grow more crops and allow larger herds of livestock to graze. The loss of woodlands and their vast root systems allowed soil to erode into streams and creeks, suffocating aquatic organisms and carrying large amounts of sediment downstream (Figure 3.2). Pesticides came into use to combat the insect pests that became adept at targeting just one or two crops. Eventually, the large-scale use of pesticides introduced poisons into our soil and water, leading to further problems as these dangerous toxins moved up through the food chain.

IMPLICATIONS FOR THE FUTURE

Different cultures are still discovering the food crops of other regions. As these new foods make their way to our gardens and kitchen tables, they will affect the diets of future generations and cultures. Some South American grains and cereals are also just now being introduced to our markets. One example is the

Figure 3.2 An Iowa farm shows signs of soil erosion after a heavy storm. Soil erosion reduces the quality of the soil and also harms rivers and creeks that receive the run-off soil.

Andean grain quinoa (*Chenopodium quinoa*). Quinoa provides protein for millions of people in the Andes, where the crop thrives despite the high altitude, extreme cold, and high winds. The ancient Incas considered quinoa sacred. Containing high levels of all the essential amino acids, it may provide a more balanced food than wheat, rice, corn, sorghum, or millet.[5]

Famines, like those associated with the potato in Ireland, illustrate the danger of depending heavily on a single crop. As crop monocultures become ever more vulnerable to disease, we have begun to realize the importance of agricultural techniques emphasizing biodiversity—some of which were practiced hundreds and thousands of years ago. Preserving the genes of the wild relatives of long-domesticated plants will also help provide a safety net. The agricultural and scientific knowledge of indigenous people around the world will be critical to our future global food security.

Ethnobotanists recognize that for centuries humans have observed each other's cultures and adopted their plants for food, textiles, medicines, and the like. But there was a missing link. We were taking the plant, but we were not taking into account the plant's relationship with its own ecosystem. Ironically, native people had grown these same foods for centuries without destroying their natural habitats or depleting their own food supply. By studying the agricultural techniques of indigenous people and their ability to understand the complex relationships that plants have with one another in an ecosystem, the ethnobotanist plays an important role in promoting healthier

Food Origins

Where do some of your favorite foods come from? Often the tastes we associate most with a particular culture come from afar. At some point in history a new plant, new seed, or new fruit was introduced into a region that slowly changed the area's cultural flavor.

TOMATO

Native to Mexico, the tomato (*Lycopersicon esculentum*) is also found in the Andes of Peru, where botanical geneticists still search for wild relatives that might help strengthen the genetic quality of our modern crops. The tomato is perhaps the single plant that Americans most associate with Italian cuisine, but before the explorations of the Americas, Italians did not create or serve tomato sauce on their meals. The Spaniards introduced the tomato to Italy in the mid-sixteenth century. In the United States, it was even later before tomatoes were enjoyed, since they were thought to be poisonous until the nineteenth century.

farming methods and improved methods in our efforts to feed the world.

Today, the increasing concern about food supplies in third-world countries has led to an increased interest in indigenous food varieties. Recording and documenting local foods has long been an ethnobotanical practice. Now those same ethnobotanists are also focusing on collecting the genetic resources of the wild relatives of our major crops. Preserving both the gene pools of these historic species and the plant knowledge of indigenous cultures could help transform the industry of farming back to a healthy, sustainable way of life that compliments our natural ecosystems.

CHILI PEPPER

Chili peppers (*Capsicum annuum*) transformed world cuisine through a simple navigational accident. In search of black pepper for Europeans, explorers traveled abroad in search of new sources of the spice. No pepper was found in the New World, but chili peppers were one of the new spices found in Latin America.

Chilies provide the zest that we associate with Indian, Chinese, and Southeast Asian cuisine. Capsaicin, the fiery ingredient in peppers, is believed to be an effective anti-inflammatory drug for the treatment of arthritis. Like so many plants, chilies may soon have as significant a medical impact as they have culinary influence.

CHOCOLATE

Who can imagine a world without chocolate? One of the world's most popular desserts comes from the cacao plant (*Theobroma cacao*). The name "chocolate" comes from the Aztecs of Mexico who considered chocolate a "gift from the gods." When chocolate made its way to Europe, this dark treat became an important trade item.

4 Plants as Medicine

Let food be our medicine and medicine be our food.
—Hippocrates (460 BC–380 BC)
Greek physician

Plants as Medicine

When confronted with an illness, indigenous people have always looked to the plants of their environment for their cures and gathered wild plants as medicine. Whereas your own medicine may come from the local drugstore, many of the medicines you are prescribed still contain drugs from a natural plant source. Native cultures had no such store to visit when they were sick. Instead, they depended on the healing plants of the fields, woodlands, marshes, deserts, and seashores they lived on.

Finding the right plants, however, was often a matter of trial and error. It is not hard to imagine that many natives died chewing on the wrong plant roots or drinking a toxic tea steeped from leaves or bark in an effort to stave off illness. When a **poultice** or infusion did appear to help a sick patient, the plant and its remedy would become widely known and used. Undoubtedly these were costly experiments, but over the ages the natives collected and passed on their cures through their own particular method of record keeping: oral storytelling.

Because natives resorted to storytelling rather than writing, ancient remedies that did end up in contemporary books were likely passed along through the interactions between natives and early European settlers, missionaries, soldiers, and trappers. In America's history, important and potentially life-saving information was preserved in the journals and letters of these men and women after Indian medicine men had shared their knowledge with them. Many native remedies found their way into our earliest pharmaceutical books in this way.

POISON OR POTENTIAL?

In the dense, humid jungles of eastern Ecuador lives a tribe of indigenous people called the Waorani. Skilled naturalists, they depend on the rain forest for much of their diet. Their relationship with the environment is impressive. The Waorani are able to interpret and anticipate natural phenomena like flowering cycles, pollination, fruit and seed dispersal, and the preferred foods of the forest animals the Waorani depend on. What excites ethnobotanists most are the tribe's extraction, manipulation, and use of the chemical compounds found in plants.[6]

Consider the dart or arrow poison, **curare**. From the *Chondrodendron* or *Strychnos* vines, its active ingredients are found in the bark. The chemicals obtained from this plant are so powerful that physicians use a derivative of *Chondrodendron tomentosum* as a muscle relaxant during surgery.[7]

There are immense numbers of chemicals obtained from plants for a variety of reasons, but the difficult preparation of curare and toxins like it suggest that their uses would never have been apparent just by observing the plant itself. An unusual intellect is required since the preparation of this poison is extremely complex. It is for this reason that ethnobotanists recognize **shamans**, or native healers, as highly skilled practitioners of medicine.

In the case of curare, the plant's bark is scraped off and placed in a funnel-shaped leaf compress suspended between two hunting spears. Cold water is then percolated through the compress while the drippings are collected in a ceramic pot. The collected dark-colored drippings are slowly heated over a fire and brought to a frothy boil numerous times until the fluid thickens. Then a period of cooling and reheating takes place until a thick gummy layer forms on the surface of the liquid. After the thick surface layer is removed, darts or arrow tips are dipped into the fluid and then slowly dried by a fire. What is most startling about the discovery of the uses of curare? When pieces of the parent plant are swallowed, the substance is harmless. But when the bark is processed in this specific way and injected intramuscularly, the dark substance is deadly. The knowledge possessed by indigenous people like the Waorani is sought by both ethnobotanists and the medical community.

Many so-called primitive peoples have learned to create complicated chemical preparations, sometimes involving ingredients from more than one plant. Through their own systems of teaching and learning, native people have been able to determine that different chemical **compounds** in relatively small concentrations can improve the effect of just one single compound.

The observations that the shaman makes are the result of adaptations of highly specialized skills that arise from a view of nature and the universe in which humans are perceived as a part of the whole. Ethnobotanists believe that it is this unique perspective that has enabled the shaman to mimic the intricate balance of the ecosystem in which he lives.

THE THREAT TO MEDICAL TREASURES

The widespread destruction of our natural ecosystems along with the threatened and real extinction of numerous plant and animal species continues before we know even the most basic facts about what we are losing. The tremendous botanical resources of tropical forests have already provided tangible medical advances, yet only 1% of the known plant and animal species have been thoroughly examined for their medicinal potentials while the world's rain forest destruction goes on.

We know that wild plant species can serve medicine in many ways. Extracts from plants can be used directly as drugs (Figure 4.1). Whether simply to combat a headache or to treat something far more serious, like Parkinson's disease, medicines obtained from plants have provided modern society with a variety of cures and pain relievers:

- Quinine, an aid in the cure of malaria, is an alkaloid extracted from the bark of the cinchona tree found in Latin America and Africa.

- The rosy periwinkle *Catharanthus roseus* from the African island of Madagascar provides several antitumor agents and aids in the treatment of pediatric leukemia and Hodgkin's disease.

Figure 4.1 A plant biotechnologist extracts artemisinin from wormwood leaves. Artemisinin is a drug used to treat malaria.

- The wild yam *Dioscorea alata* from Mexico and Guatemala has provided us with diosgenin, which is used in the manufacture of birth control pills. For a long time, yams were the world's only known source of diosgenin.

The chemicals found in plants made our natural ecosystems the first laboratories. By studying the chemicals in individual species of plants, scientists learned how to artificially synthesize drug compounds. Aspirin was created from willow tree *(Salix)* extracts found in the rain forest. Neostigmine, a chemical derived from the Calabar bean *(Physostigma venmosum)* and used in the past to treat glaucoma, led to the creation of synthetic insecticides. Creating a synthetic drug in a modern laboratory is very expensive. Since the chemical structures of most natural drugs are so complex, extraction from the actual plant is often less costly.

Plants serve as research tools as well. The compounds in some plants have enabled researchers to better understand how cancer cells grow. Other compounds have served as testing agents for potentially harmful food and drug products. Plants may offer a solution to a safer contraceptive. Approximately 4,000 plant species have already been shown to offer contraceptive capabilities.[8] The forest may also provide a safer pesticide for farmers. Some wild potatoes have leaves that produce a sticky substance that traps and kills predatory insects. This natural self-defense mechanism could potentially reduce the need for using pesticides on potatoes, preventing some dangerous toxins from entering the environment.

SHAMANS AND INDIGENOUS PEOPLES

It is estimated that one out of every four prescription drugs was discovered by ethnobotanical studies of medicinal plant uses by indigenous people.[9] Plants have always been a source of medicine for every culture in the world. Medicinal teas, poultices, ointments, comfrey leaves, coriander, sage, sarsaparilla root, and hot peppers have all been used to relieve pain. The stems and leaves of banana and aloe plants have been used to treat burns and blisters. Many of these ancient remedies developed into the modern medicines that we use today. A pain-relieving substance called salicin was extracted from willow and birch bark, giving people an early form of aspirin. Another of the earliest salicin-based medicines was a myrtle leaf treatment made by ancient Egyptians to soothe back pain in 1500 B.C. Ethnobotanists believe that the chemical components of plants used in indigenous healing rites could be the foundation for new life-improving drugs or possibly even a cure for ravaging diseases like cancers or AIDS.

For thousands of years, indigenous groups have made extensive use of their plant knowledge to meet their health needs. Shamans were the first medical specialists in indigenous communities, and their traditional methods are known to be effective in treating both physical and psychological ailments. The World Health Organization (WHO) estimates that 80% of the people in developing countries still rely on traditional medicine for their primary health-care needs. Without money or faith in modern medicine, indigenous people still depend on shamans, herbal healers, and native plants for their survival. Shamans also play a crucial role in helping ethnobotanists discover the potential uses of plants (Figure 4.2). There is an urgency to preserve this unique source of information, but the cultural survival of this ancient medicine is seriously threatened as developed nations, huge corporations, and others invade and systematically destroy the forests where the individuals safeguarding this information live.

THE ORIGINS OF FOLK MEDICINE

Plants have always been available to people and have therefore been a constant part of our diet and healing practices. Every continent has its own kind of folk medicine; indeed, every tribe has its own. The use of plants as **hallucinogens** dates back at least 10,000 years; the use of plants for medicines probably

Figure 4.2 An ethnobotanist talks with a shaman's apprentice in Suriname, a country in northern South America. Because shamans have a vast knowledge of native plant life, they are vital resources for the ethnobotanist.

dates back even farther to the most ancient hunter-gatherer societies.

As cures were discovered, descriptions of a plant, its location within its habitat, and its medicinal properties would be passed by word of mouth and storytelling. This practice would become known as folk medicine. The term "folk medicine" is often misused. Folk medicine has been used to describe the medicine practiced by people who have no access to professional medical services, suggesting that those who practice folk medicine are settling for a lesser quality of medicine. Or that people who practice folk medicine simply lack the means to acquire more sophisticated means of healing themselves.

The idea that folk medicine is inferior to modern medicine is a view that ethnobotanists are trying to change. In fact, field research shows that folk medicines are sophisticated and complex and that the indigenous cultures in possession of this knowledge have important lessons to teach the modern world.

NATURE'S HEALING PHARMACY

The Babylonians imported myrrh for medicinal use by 3000 B.C. Mention of medicinal plants occurred in the earliest Chinese monograph (2700 B.C.) and in India (1500 B.C. in a religious text called the Rig-Veda). Physicians like Hippocrates used plant medicines, as did the Greek Theophrastus and Dioscorides. Dioscorides's *Materia Medica* was the classic textbook of plant medicines for nearly 1,500 years, and works by Pliny the Elder also contained valuable information on botanical medicine.

The first chemicals used to lower body temperature during fever were from willow plants (*Salix*) and *Cinchona* (a source of quinine). In the 1880s the cocaine plant was used as an anesthetic for delicate eye surgery. As late as the 1970s, 25% of the drugs in use in North America and Europe contained some plant extract or plant derivative. Although that number has decreased due to replacement by synthetic drugs, plants are still extremely valuable sources for some of our most powerful medicines.

No one argues that naturally occurring plants are responsible for many of our prescription drugs, but according to *National Geographic* (Swerdlow, April 2000) the **Food and Drug Administration** (FDA) has approved fewer than 12 new plant-based pharmaceuticals in the past 40 years. Despite the promise of plant chemicals, we still are not tapping into all the substances that may be available in nature, since such a small percentage of the world's vegetation has been investigated for its therapeutic value.

THE CHEMICAL PROPERTIES OF PLANTS

We know that plant shape, form, and function differ greatly among the approximately 250,000 varieties of flowering species. It is also safe to assume that the medicinal properties found within each plant probably differ as well. That same diversity has never been duplicated in the animal world, and no animal, not even a human working in a sophisticated laboratory, has ever been able to produce even a small fraction of the chemicals produced by plants.

What causes the diversity of chemicals found within plants and why might a plant produce chemicals? We know that all green plants utilize carbon dioxide and sunlight to go through the food-making process of photosynthesis. But not all plants

The Growing Popularity of Medicinal Herbs

According to the government conservation organization Plant Conservation Alliance, the demand for nonprescription medicinal herbs derived from native North American plants is thriving. As many as 175 different species of plants are now being collected from the wild for a $3 billion commercial market in the United States and overseas. Among the plants in high demand are goldenseal (*Hydrastis canadensis*) and ginseng (*Panax quinquefolius*). Just the harvests of these two species from our eastern forests have resulted in the loss of nearly 100 million individual plants during the past few years.

And the demand is only growing. Until recently, natural herbs were considered only an alternative to traditional medicine, but today many doctors often recommend their use.

What will become of our native plants and their habitats if these plants continue to be collected at this rate? Until methods are created to farm these plants on a commercial scale, steps must be taken to ensure that any harvest that continues is done on a sustainable basis to ensure that the natural ecosystems where these plants exist are not plundered.

have the same chemicals, so it is unlikely that photosynthesis has a role in the creation of chemicals in plants. So why does a plant produce a chemical? What purpose does the chemical serve the plant?

Some botanists believe the answer to that question might be found by examining how a plant protects itself from attack or how a plant deals with competition within its habitat. Unlike animals, plants cannot move from one place to another to carry out reproductive activities. Instead, plants rely on animals, wind, water, and other environmental factors to move their seeds and pollen. Plants cannot escape an enemy. A plant's inability to move may be the primary reason it produces chemicals. Plant chemicals are a defense strategy.

Interactions between plants and animals are not necessarily harmless. Plants do have a way to fight back. From a plant's point of view, the grinding molars of a giraffe or the sucking mouthparts of a cicada pose the same threat as a stalking leopard has to a gazelle on the Serengeti plains. Because plants cannot flee their predators they have become specialists in a certain kind of biochemical warfare.

The relationship is not totally antagonistic. Plant chemicals can reward animals, too. Plant nectar provides an important food source for many birds, bats, and insects in exchange for their work at pollinating a flower or carrying seeds to a new location. But the vast majority of chemicals produced by plants are designed to repel or poison animals that attempt to destroy them. Those same chemical agents that plants create and use against animals have profound implication for our medicines.

The useful chemicals of plants, combined with their food production and their immobility, make it easy to understand why plants have always been critical for human survival. Since indigenous people have become experts at using the plant resources around them, ethnobotanists go directly to the source to learn more about the medicinal properties of plants.

TODAY AND THE FUTURE

Since the early 1990s, there has been a growing interest in the identification and preservation of plants, since they are the source for many of today's drugs. Pharmaceutical companies are especially interested in exploring parts of the world where plant medicine remains the predominant form of dealing with illness. The jungles and rain forests of South America, for example, have an extraordinary diversity of plant species, each of which has the potential to provide a unique medical use. Many of these regions are still unexplored, leaving these potentially useful species in danger of disappearing forever as vital ecosystems are lost to encroaching development.

With the renewed interest in using ancient plants as medicinal agents, ethnobotanists work with shamans to identify and collect plants utilized to treat diseases. Ethnobotanists are working today with physicians to research and develop products that can be of use to pharmaceutical companies. This is a glimpse of ethnobotany today.

One of the greatest economic values of ethnobotany may lie in the area of folk medicines. Indigenous healers first discovered many of these drugs. Whether you call them shamans, sorcerers, herbalists, or witch doctors, they are responsible for making available some of our most potent medicines. These medicines have come from native ecosystems—discovered by those living closest to the plants.

But since these medicines come from plants that still represent just a minor segment of the world's flora, any practical strategy for expanding our knowledge of these living pharmaceutical factories must include ethnobotanical research.

Ethnobotanists know that if we are to take advantage of traditional knowledge we must do more than preserve the plants. We must save the cultures that are immersed in their ecosystems. The intellectual achievements of indigenous people suggest that the biggest challenge for ethnobotanists lies not in the identification and removal of natural organisms but in the adaptation and promotion of a wholly different way of living on Earth.

When all the trees have been cut down, when all the animals have been hunted, when all the waters are polluted, when all the air is unsafe to breathe, only then will you discover you cannot eat money.
—Native American (Cree tribe) prophecy

The Relationship Between Native North Americans and Plants

The primal, buzzing sound of a snake rattle vibrating under the scrub brush beside your feet is enough to stop anyone in his tracks—just as nature designed it. If you choose to stick around long enough to look for the source of the sound, you may be rewarded with the sight of a large-scaled, thick-bodied reptile. Slowly coiling on a bed of leaves, the snake would raise its head and upper body into a characteristic defensive pose as its dark tongue rhythmically darts, trying to smell the threat it senses from your presence.

Today we know that most people can safely watch this snake from a short distance. Few people encounter rattlesnakes in the wild, and fewer still ever suffer the effects of a venomous snake-bite. But suppose the worst did happen. Suppose the snake never heard your approach. Without time to react to you, a rattlesnake would not rattle its tail in alarm. Without that danger signal, you and the snake could meet ... with unpleasant consequences.

Fortunately in this country today, a person who is bitten by a rattlesnake is probably hiking and probably has a cell phone. Once help arrives, ambulances or helicopters can swiftly get a patient to the closest hospital. There, doctors can quickly administer treatments, such as antivenin, antibiotics, and painkillers.

But what if it was the year 1805? What if you were hunting alone for jackrabbits in the hot summer sun? After a long morning, you stop beneath a flat rock outcrop to crouch in the cool shade. The snake does not hear you and you do not notice it stretched out in the shade. As you reach for a handhold along the flaky shale to pull yourself out of the sun you feel something brush against you. *Now* you see the snake. But it is too late. Within moments, the tip of your finger starts to burn and shortly after, your hand starts to swell. What will you do?

If you were Native American and had listened closely to the stories of your father or grandfathers, you would know to look for a plant called snakeroot (Figure 5.1). This is one of the plants

Figure 5.1 Seneca snakeroot is the common name of the plant *Polygala senega*.

you had grown up with, and it would provide you with the latest in medical discoveries—the best treatment available to you after years of experiments by tribal leaders.

LIVING IN BALANCE WITH NATURE

Like indigenous peoples around the world, Native Americans practiced the philosophy of living in balance with all life on Earth. They long ago possessed a sophisticated understanding of nature derived from thousands of years of observing the relationships between living things and their environment. Their own relationship with the plants around them was deep and personal. It was both life-saving and life-sustaining—a relationship designed to feed the body *and* the soul.

Native Americans saw themselves as a part of nature, not separate from it. They believed the animals were their brothers, the plants their sisters. A relationship with the natural world was emphasized over a desire or need to control nature. Their unfenced gardens grew food alongside the wild plants they foraged and the wildlife they revered.

With this intimate knowledge of plants, the lives of the natives revolved around the seasons and the natural bounties each month provided. While scavenging in the wild, native peoples made sure to protect the wild plants that provided them with food, herbal remedies, and dyes. The forest and fields were their first gardens and eventually became extensions of their cultivated gardens. Wild berries, seeds, nuts, roots, and fruits were paramount to their survival and culture. Even early wildlife management techniques were practiced to ensure that plenty of plants flourished for the wildlife the natives depended on for their food, clothing, tools, and ceremonies. When land did have to be cleared for crops and villages, care was taken to preserve plenty of other natural habitats to sustain them in the future (Figure 5.2).

Figure 5.2 This drawing of the Native American village of Secota was made in the 1580s by John White, an English explorer and artist. The villagers of Secota grew a variety of plants, including corn and sunflowers.

THE FIRST FARMERS

The first farmers on our continent were Native Americans. Farming brought an important change to the native way of life. It made sedentary life possible and led to home building, the growth of villages, and increases in population. Despite these benefits, farming was still often practiced only to augment the wild food that was secured through hunting, fishing, and foraging.

Most North Americans had a matriarchal society. The special power of creating life and giving birth was something only the women could share with "Mother Earth." The Native Americans recognized and acknowledged this gift. While men were the hunters and defenders of the tribe, women were the gatherers and were therefore probably responsible for the development of the original farms. Women most likely were the first to collect plants and harvest wild seeds (Figure 5.3). And, except for the boys who stood guard at the garden or old men who did heavy tilling, the women were responsible for most gardening chores.

Animals were held in high esteem in Native American cultures for the gifts they provided, but they often took a toll on the garden crops—deer, birds, and rodents especially. Young tribal boys held the responsibility of "guarding" the crops by perching on a platform beside the garden to discourage the animals or to hunt them. Whenever animals did damage the crops, the animals might be harvested for food and clothing. But one animal was usually spared, despite its capacity for damage.

According to legend, the intelligent, bold crow was believed to have brought the single most important plant to the Native Americans: the first grain of corn *(Zea mays)*. Corn (or maize) is perhaps the Native Americans' greatest contribution to the world's food resources. Different tribal dialects had words in their language for corn such as "our life," "it sustains us," or "giver of life." As the importance of corn grew within a tribe, the

Figure 5.3 An Apache woman is seen harvesting wheat with a hand sickle in this photograph from 1906.

plant became the center of art and religious life of many tribes. Ceremonies were performed on behalf of the plant and its life-sustaining qualities. The Iroquois people alone had more than 23 different recipes for maize.

THE THREE SISTERS

Cooperation between plants was well understood by the natives and they used this information to their benefit. While the plants widely used by various tribes numbered in the thousands, three plants were selected as the foundation of early Native American agriculture. Over time these three plants were improved enough to be hand-grown with relative ease and in sufficient quantity to sustain the lives of the natives as well as provide a harvest for storage. Once they had enough food to live above the needs of daily subsistence, there was leisure time to establish settled, agricultural societies.

These three plants were corn, beans, and squash, better known as the Three Sisters. Corn was the center of the garden. The corn provided staple foods such as maize, hominy, and cake, but its vital role in the garden was in supporting the beans and squash. The Three Sisters technique, or three crops garden, required that the corn be planted among varieties of beans and squash. The relationship between the three plants as they grew together helped retain moisture, replenish and maintain soil conditions, and control weeds. The tall corn stalks provided support for the climbing beans. The climbing beans helped fix nitrogen in the soil for the corn. The spreading squash plants shaded, cooled, and controlled the weeds in the soil below the corn and beans.

The relationship between the Three Sisters held other benefits too. Botanical differences between the three species guaranteed that they would not all succumb to a single pest attack or weather-related catastrophe. The natives recognized that the growth habits of each of the Three Sisters were as different as their nutritional requirements. Beans could survive during a cloudy and cool summer season that would halt the growth of corn and most squash. The stormy summer winds that mowed down corn stalks and tore the large, thin leaves of squash would not bother the small, tough leaves and vining stems of the beans. And finally, the deep-rooted corn could withstand both drought and the sudden squalls that might wash out the less well-rooted beans and squash.

The spiritual relationship of the Three Sisters was sacred and nearly universal among the settled, agricultural native people of North America. The Cherokee version of how corn came to feed the Indians is a typical story among North American tribes.

The Origin of Corn

In almost every native nation there is a story about the origin of the corn plant. Where did these stories come from? The traditional belief is that the corn itself spoke to tribe members. Native lore recognizes that human life is dependent on the plants and that those plants have an awareness of their surroundings and therefore deserve our respect. In native stories, plants interact directly with people, talking freely and entering the human realm.

Southern New England Indians described maize (or corn) as a gift from Cautantowwit, a god associated with southwestern direction. Many other tribes in this region believed the first corn was delivered by the raven—a bird held in high esteem and not to be harmed, even if it caused damage to a carefully managed cornfield. The Algonquin legends recall corn as a reward sent by the Great Spirit through a person of his choice.

The story of the Coming of Corn, belonging to the Cherokee of North Carolina, shares details similar to many other Native American stories. In essence, it tells how a young boy's grandmother came to be the first stalk of corn after sacrificing her life so that the corn would live and feed her people. In this version, the grandmother tells her grandson to clear away a patch of ground on the south side of their lodge after she has died. He is told to drag her body over that ground seven times and then bury her in that patch of earth. She tells the young boy that if he does as she says, he will see her again and he will be able to feed his people.

The grandson did as he was told and wherever he dragged his grandmother's body and a drop of her blood fell, a small plant grew. As the plants grew taller it seemed he could hear his grandmother's voice whispering in the leaves. In time, the plants grew very tall and the long tassels at the top of each plant reminded the boy of his grandmother's long hair. When the ears of corn finally formed on each plant his, grandmother's promise had come true. Though she had gone from the Earth, she would be with the boy's people forever as the corn plant to feed them.

THE DOCTRINE OF SIGNATURES

How did the Native Americans know which plants cured which ills? One method of discovering what ailment a plant might cure was to simply look at the plant. A theory of medicinal plant lore called the "doctrine of signatures" suggests that plants that hold potential cures actually show visual clues to their uses. In other words, people who believe in this theory believe that the shape or color of a particular plant (or part of it) would give an indication to what it might cure.

For example, in the case of snakebite, natives would most likely have first looked for a plant resembling the long, twisted shape of a snake. That is how the snaking roots of Virginia snakeroot and other members of the milkwort family became a well-known antidote for venom. The roots of the snakeroot were chewed and then applied directly onto the bite as a poultice. Because of its known benefit as a snakebite remedy, the roots of the snakeroot plant were often harvested in autumn and carried in leather pouches for just such an emergency.

Following the doctrine of signatures, a plant could help soothe an inflamed eye if you found a flower that resembled the eye of a deer. A tea made from gnarled wood was believed to control convulsions. Liver disorders would be treated with hepatica, or liverleaf, whose leaves are shaped like the human liver, and so on.

TOP TEN PLANTS USED BY NATIVE AMERICANS

Today, botanists can classify over 2,500 species of plants that were used by Native Americans for medicinal, food, fiber, and ceremonial purposes. And while corn, beans, and squash were central to the garden and the ceremonies honoring food, the following is a list, with descriptions, of the ten plants recognized for their broadest uses by the largest number of tribes. The list originally appeared in *Native American Ethnobotany* by Daniel E. Moerman.

- *Thuja plicata,* **western red cedar**—used to make cough medicine, chewing gum, green dye, baskets, and broth.

- *Prunus virginiana,* **common chokecherry**—used to treat sore throats and to control diarrhea.

- *Urtica dioca,* **stinging nettle**—rubbed on the body to treat aches and pains; dried, peeled stems used as twine.

- *Yucca baccata,* **banana yucca**—used to treat heartburn, as a hair wash, and to make string and shoes; fruit soaked and cooked into a syrup.

- *Cornus sericea,* **red osier dogwood**—used to soothe eye pain and prevent infection; berries are edible; bark burned to create smoke during ceremonies.

- *Heracleum maximum,* **common cowparsnip**—used as medicine for colds and sore throats, flower buds eaten with honey, and roots used to make a yellow dye.

- *Rhus trilobata,* **skunkbush sumac**—used to treat smallpox sores, dried fruits made into jams, and berries soaked in water to make lemonade-like drink.

- *Pseudotsuga menziesii,* **Douglas fir**—used to make snowshoes, to flavor bear meat, and placed inside moccasins to keep feet dry.

- *Bettual payrifera,* **paper birch**—burned to make smoked fish and meat; wood used to make canoes, toboggans, and snowshoes; bark used to waterproof roofs.

- *Populus balsamifera,* **balsam poplar**—used on sores, to prevent infection by parasites, and to make saddles.

Come forth into the light of things. Let Nature be your teacher.
—William Wordsworth (1770–1850)
English poet

How Plants Create Cultures

Can you imagine the Vikings of Scandinavia without their huge sailing vessels or the northeastern woodland tribes without their longhouses? How would the Shipibo Indians of the Amazon rain forest hunt without their hand-carved blowguns? What kind of legacy would the desert Navajos leave us if there were no dyes to create the vibrant colors found in their hand-woven rugs?

Much attention is focused on the conservation of plants for their keystone role in the function of ecosystems, and for important medicinal purposes, and rightly so. Plants have served us throughout history is so many ways. But what happens when civilizations lose their access to the plants that formed their culture?

Consider the mystery of Easter Island (Figure 6.1). At only 64 square miles (166 square km), located amid the Pacific Ocean 2,000 miles (3,200 km) west of the nearest continent of South American, this storied island, with its huge stone-carved heads, is considered the world's most isolated piece of habitable land.

The subtropical mild climate and fertile volcanic soil should have made this small piece of land a miniature paradise, remote from problems that plagued the rest of world. For several centuries, apparently it was. But on Easter in 1722, Dutch explorer Jacob Roggeveen landed on the island to find a wasteland, not a paradise.

As Roggeveen approached the land, he first noticed that the Polynesians, famous for their seafaring skills and large outrigger canoes, were instead approaching his ship in small, fragile vessels, or simply swimming out to greet him and his men. When the Dutchmen made landfall there was not a single tree or bush over 10 feet (3 m) tall, unlike the lush tropical islands they had surveyed in the past. There were no native animals larger than an insect, even though other Polynesian islands were home to

Figure 6.1 The statues on Easter Island were carved from volcanic rock by the islanders between A.D. 1100 and 1600. Construction of the statues ceased after the total deforestation of the island.

numerous species of land birds, bats, snails, and lizards. Even the human population, estimated at about 2,000, was low.

An explanation for what happened to the people and the plants that once created an island of magnificent statues remained a mystery for several hundred more years until ethnobotanists and archeologists unraveled the history of Easter Island.

Tens of thousands of pollen grains, found in columns of sediment beneath island marshes and ponds, were analyzed and it was determined that the earliest evidence of human activity dates back as far as A.D. 300 to A.D. 400. The statues most likely were carved and erected between A.D. 1100 and 1600, when the human population was about 7,000 or perhaps as large as 20,000.

Originally, Easter Island was covered by a subtropical forest of trees and woody bushes shading a ground cover of shrubs, herbs, ferns, and grasses. The dominant trees were Hauhau and island palms, which the scientists believed were used to build large canoes and help move and erect the statues.

Further excavations of the island's landscape provided evidence of the islanders' surprising diet. Instead of shallow-water fish, one-third of all bones uncovered in analyzed trash heaps were from ocean-dwelling porpoises. The significance of this discovery meant that these people did indeed once have access to large trees that were made into deep ocean-going vessels that could overtake a fast-swimming mammal.

Clearly, something had happened on Easter Island that changed this culture from a flourishing community of boat builders and deep-sea fishermen into sparse grassland—one where the declining populations had no way to fish, little wood left to burn for heat or cooking, and a food supply that was rapidly disappearing. The seriousness of the predicament that the inhabitants of Easter Island found themselves in was also uncovered in the island's excavated trash heaps.

In addition to the porpoise, fish, and bird bones, buried among the remains of the islanders' food supplies were the bones of humans. This discovery painted a bleak picture of what probably happened as the islanders used up their natural resources. The islanders began to cannibalize one another as the island's vegetation disappeared.

It is believed that by the seventeenth century, most of Easter Island's plants were extinct. In time, all native species of land birds were extinct. The first Polynesians had once found themselves on an island that provided everything they needed for comfortable living. As their populations grew they began erecting stone statues as a sign of status, wealth, and power. But eventually, the island's growing population began cutting the forests more rapidly than the trees could regenerate. As the forest disappeared, so went the timber and rope to transport and erect the statues, and build fires. Without the plants, the birds disappeared. Without the wood for boats, they could no longer travel to sea for food.

With food in short supply, chiefs and priests could no longer keep the once complex society running. Local chaos replaced centralized government and a warrior class took over. In time, many of the great statues were toppled to the ground in warfare, and the history of the island, even to those who lived there, became lost. When Roggeveen landed on Easter Island early in the 1720s, no one who lived there was able to describe what had happened to their own ancestors.

Easter Island is a drastic example of what happens to a society that does not use sustainable methods when harvesting its natural resources. When the products of the island ecosystems were depleted, the culture was lost forever.

Historical maps of our world illustrate the passages taken by cultures that crafted ships from the plants of their region. Those plants enabled men to sail themselves and their food crops around the world, and in doing so, they ultimately altered the ecosystems and indigenous cultures of every land they encountered.

Plants were sought for every purpose, such as for the adhesive qualities of their gum or sap. Woven cords and twines were manufactured from plants. Chemicals from plants were altered into deadly poisons and used for weapons that were as dangerous as any gun or knife available at the time. Bark and hollowed trees became vital containers for storing food or carrying water great distances (Figure 6.2). The various plants used for these purposes allowed people to travel away from water and establish villages in new settlements. Dyes from plants were used as body

Figure 6.2 A canoe has been dug out from a single tree by the Matses Indian tribe in the Amazon rain forest of Peru.

paints and tattoos, defining social status and ceremonial rites. The dyes improved the appearance of textiles and woven objects and helped identify specific cultures and artisans.

THE RELIGIOUS USE OF PLANTS

Plants have always been sought to alter man's mind and spirit. Perhaps the most controversial use of plants throughout history has been the use of plants for ritualistic or religious purposes, or for illegal or recreational purposes. Both the ethnobotanist and the medical world are interested in the chemical properties of plants as a source of possible treatments or cures of disease. But the ethnobotanist is also interested in the chemical properties of plants as they relate to the worldview of indigenous people.

The use of plants in religious ceremonies is widespread and often provides insight into how a culture views death or the afterlife. Even in our industrialized country, flowers play an important role in harvest and holiday celebrations as well as weddings and funerals. Throughout the world, plants are seen as symbols of spiritual power, and many cultures gain access to what they perceive as the afterlife by ingesting plant parts. These ceremonies and experiences are as important to them as any church or temple service is to its members in this country.

The Quechua Indians of Ecuador boil the ayahuasca vine (*Banisteriopsis caapi*) in water before drinking the tea, with the intent of releasing their spirit to wander the world. Before their spirit returns to their body, the Quechua reportedly experience mental telepathy and the ability to forecast the future.

Native American cultures have been documented using a derivative of the peyote cactus *(Lophophora)* since the mid-sixteenth century to induce colorful visions and create a sense of well-being. The tips or heads of the peyote cactus are cut and dried into "buttons," which when mixed with saliva and swallowed, produce strong hallucinations. During the past several centuries, peyote use among Native Americans has risen and fallen as the United States government has alternately tried to control or condemn its use. As recently as 1993, the Religious Freedom Act allowed peyote use in the Native American Church as part of their religious sacrament.[10]

While the use of hallucinogens by indigenous cultures is widespread, the concept seems foreign to most of us in Western cultures. But we use plants on a daily basis to gently alter our moods. Among the less controversial substances we ingest from plants to help us wake in the morning, get through our hectic day, or relax in the evening are coffee, tobacco, wine, and chocolate. In fact, under many circumstances, these substances are used to enhance our social functions.

Can a Shaman Really Heal the Sick?

Well-known ethnobotanists Michael J. Balick and Magnus Zethelius have spent years studying the work of shamans in native villages, and they believe these "medicine men" do have the ability to improve the condition of individuals who are ill. In addition, they have observed what they refer to as "healings," not only in remote villages, but also under the watchful eyes of numerous physicians in clinical settings.

In one particular case study, a young man from the Orinoco Valley of Colombia was brought to a medical clinic one day after having been bitten by *Bothrops,* a venomous snake. When the patient was admitted, he was pale, confused, and delirious. Vital statistics such as his blood pressure, pulse, respiratory rate, and temperature all indicated a very serious reaction to the snake venom. The man also had severe swelling and purple discoloration of the skin near the site of the wound, with a significant amount of blood in his urine.

The doctors immediately administered antivenim serum, but the patient's condition only worsened. A Guahibo shaman who happened to be present asked permission to administer a traditional "smoke-blowing" treatment, which involved blowing tobacco smoke on the patient's extremities while chanting a call similar to the song of a nocturnal bird. Balick and Zethelius describe the patient as becoming relaxed as his vital signs returned to normal, though the doctors treating the young man described him as still remaining in a toxic state. Within a few days the man's condition improved and he survived the bite.

The attending physicians acknowledged that the antivenin serum alone had never produced such a drastic improvement and allowed that the traditional treatment by the shaman indeed had an effect on the patient. Balick and Zethelius concluded that the man's strong belief and trust in shamanistic practices enhanced his return to good health.

CONTROVERSIAL PLANT USE

In most Polynesian cultures, kava *(Piper methysticum)* is served to welcome visitors or deflect social tensions (Figure 6.3). It is an important part of the social interaction for South Pacific natives, similar to afternoon tea in Great Britain. Although the real significance of kava lies in the context in which it is served to a visitor or tribe member, drinking from the roots of this plant can still create a powerful effect on your mind and body. Kava has been described as creating a feeling of "fellowship and brotherhood," or a sense of "heightened perception, as if flying over the rain forest."[11]

Plants known to promote social tranquility or transport the participant through hallucinations are considered psychoactive plants. Whether they are used for religious awakening or gentle mood swings, their uses were not always intended to be beneficial.

Figure 6.3 Men from Viseisei village in Fiji prepare a mildly narcotic drink made from the roots of the kava plant. Kava is used in traditional ceremonies throughout the west Pacific islands.

In the eleventh century a Persian named Al-Hasan ibn al-Sabbah influenced young men intoxicated by *Cannabis* to rob for him and destroy anyone who got in the way of his mission. *Cannabis*, when dried and smoked, is better known as marijuana or hashish. Used for centuries for medicinal purposes, this controversial drug still remains a divisive subject when comparing the benefits of its medical potency (such as the relief of nausea associated with powerful chemotherapy drugs) with the allegations that its abuse may lead to an addiction to deadlier substances.

The fear in Western cultures that mild-altering drugs derived from plants might be abused implies that all of these plants are dangerous and have no place in a civilized culture. But psychoactive drugs do have an important role in traditional cultures, and ethnobotanists continue to investigate the relationship of these plant-derived drugs to indigenous people.

Like all drugs, the level of addiction or the amount of pain relief caused by any substance is related to its dose and the form in which it is taken. The coca bush *(Erythroxylum)* of South America has leaves that have been used for centuries as a source of nutrients and to stave off hunger and fatigue. But cocaine, the illegal and addictive drug that is chemically manufactured from the coca leaf, has a deservedly negative connotation—it is the center of enormous illegal trade, it corrupts governments, and it causes social instability.

The same can be said of opium, which comes from the poppy plant (*Papaver somniferum*). An Egyptian document called the Ebers Papyrus, dated around 1500 B.C., suggests that poppies were used long ago as a cure for headaches and as a sedative. Today we manufacture codeine and morphine from the alkaloids of opium poppies and use them as extremely powerful painkillers, among other uses. The drugs are available only through prescriptions and their use is strictly regulated.

While it may be necessary to protect people by limiting access to dangerous substances, it is also important to recognize that all civilizations view their surroundings in their own cultural context. It would be unfair and unwise to think of all plant-derived drugs as dangerous or without merit. For cultures that identify certain psychoactive drugs with the sacredness of their surroundings, imposing laws upon them threatens their way of life. For indigenous people, their life includes their entire ecosystem.

In *Plants, People, and Culture, The Science of Ethnobotany,* Michael J. Balick and Paul Alan Cox provide these examples:

- To stop the logging of Thai rain forests, priests wrapped saffron-colored robes around the trees and ordained the threatened trees as Buddhist monks.

- In the Southwestern United States, Navajo tribes have protested the construction of power lines through regional mountain ranges that they regard as holy.

- In Africa, the development of tourist resorts has pressed tribal elders to fight against the destruction of the land they refer to as their *Kayas*, or sacred groves.

In Western culture we may look at these attempts to resist "progress" as simple grandstanding, or some may suggest that these people have an ulterior motive. But an ethnobotanist would understand that a Native American who regarded the plants as his sisters, would react to tripping over an exposed tree root as having had a personal interaction with that particular tree. All indigenous people regard the natural world as sacred, and therefore worthy of preservation.

7 The Rain Forests of the World

Destroying rainforest for economic gain is like burning a renaissance painting to cook a meal.

—Edward O. Wilson (1929–   )
American biologist and writer

The Rain Forests of the World

IT'S "THE ECONOMY, STUPID"

When President William Jefferson Clinton was running for his first term in 1992, he taped a note to a wall in his office as a reminder of one of the most important issues in his campaign. Despite continuing human rights issues around the world, the lingering war in the Middle East, or the stunning riots in Los Angeles, Clinton knew that the key to solving all these issues was the economy. And so, on a small piece of paper he scribbled the words, "the economy, stupid," to always remind him to stay on track.

Like that prophetic note, the keys to solving the problems and creating the solutions to the continuing destruction of rain forests—the most powerful and biologically diverse natural ecosystem on the planet—are economic.

Every parcel of habitable land on Earth has, at some point in its history, been associated with indigenous people of a particular culture. Some of those cultures have been lost to time, slowly and quietly evolving into larger, more dominant cultures. Others have been **assimilated** by force. By definition, indigenous people are the descendants of the original inhabitants of the area where they live, sharing unique languages, cultures, and ancestral ties to that homeland. Some estimates place nearly 5,000 distinct cultures among the worldwide indigenous population of 250 million people. Indigenous people make up only 4% of the world's population of 6 billion people, but they represent 95% of the world's cultural diversity. [12]

Small pockets of indigenous cultures are found in every region of the world, still clinging to a traditional way of live while facing the encroachment and influences of the cultures of technically developed nations. The greatest concentrations of indigenous people remain in the great rain forests of the world.

Found on many different continents, rain forests all are located around the Earth's equator and share the common features of high year-round temperatures and high precipitation.

Regardless of the location, the dilemmas faced by the rain forests and their native cultures are the same. The Tafua forest on the Western Samoa island of Savaii is a good example. Small compared to the enormous Amazon forests of South America, this tract of jungle possesses the same unique claim as any rain forest; over one-quarter of its forest plants are found nowhere else on Earth. The tropical rain forests of the world are home to an enormous diversity of living organisms unique to only that one place. This leaves these isolated ecosystems extremely vulnerable to changes brought about by man-made habitat destruction, cultural assimilation, or even natural disaster.

When rain forest cultures can live undisturbed, or at least minimally disturbed, small indigenous tribes live out their lives much as their ancestors did thousands of years ago—with their health, their religion, and their livelihoods intricately tied to the plants and the ecosystems they are a part of.

Rain forests are destroyed for the profits they yield (Figure 7.1). Whether cut for lumber, slashed to clear land for cattle, or burned to open parcels of land for **subsistence** farming, nearly 200,000 acres of rain forest are lost each day for a quick source of income.[13] But the true wealth of the rain forest lies not in the trees that are removed or the businesses that are established in their wake. The real value of the rain forest lies in the nutrients, chemicals, and other active compounds found in the plants themselves—the plants that the indigenous cultures have used for their health and well-being for centuries.

If landowners, governments, and those living in the rain forest today were given economic reasons *not* to destroy the rain forest, the rapid destruction would most likely come to an end. Ethnobotanists have demonstrated that economic alternatives do exist. When medicinal plants, fruits, nuts, oils, and other resources like rubber, chocolate, and **chicle**, are harvested in a **sustainable** manner, the rain forests have more economic value than if its parts were simply removed. Sustainable harvesting of the rain

Figure 7.1 Smoke billows from the Amazon rain forest near the city of Sao Felix do Xingu in northern Brazil. Ranchers, soybean farmers, and loggers burn and cut down large swaths of the forest every year.

forest plants, rather than large-scale permanent destruction of the entire ecosystem, not only provides income now, but profits for generations to come.

Think of the resources of the rain forests as a new currency. The plant knowledge possessed by these indigenous people appears to be the new revenue for the preservation of the planet's rain forests. Since rain forests hold the distinction of supporting millions of plant species, the true value of these specific forests can be found among the shamans, healers, and indigenous people of each region.

With ethnobotanists serving as liaisons, major pharmaceutical companies and governments around the globe are sitting up and paying attention. World-renowned drug companies and major nations are currently funding projects to study indigenous plant knowledge and the specific plants used by the people closest to them.

WHAT IS A RAIN FOREST?

Rain forests have long represented mystery and power: a mythic link between humans and the natural world. The best known of the giant rain forests of the world are found in the Amazon basin (Figure 7.2). South America is home to the largest contiguous tropical rain forest in the world. The Amazon spreads across much of South America, including Colombia, Ecuador, Peru, Bolivia, Brazil, Venezuela, Guyana, Surinam, and French Guiana.

Any forest that receives more than seven feet (2.1 m) of rain annually is generally considered a rain forest. There are as many as 30 or 40 different types of rain forests, including evergreen lowland forests, evergreen mountain forests, tropical evergreen alluvial forests, and semi-deciduous forests.

Covering only 2% of the Earth's surface, rain forests are home to an astounding half of the world's plant and animal species. Scientists estimate that just one four-square-mile (10.4 square km) carpet of lush rain forest may contain more than 750 types of trees and 1,500 species of flowering plants.

Rain forests represent one of the six major biomes found on Earth, each the result of eons of successional changes as each ecosystem evolved into the one biome that represents its most stable stage. The rain forests are also considered the oldest ecosystems on Earth. Fossils found in the rain forests of Southeast Asia are believed to be 70 to 100 million years old.

Despite their significance, we know that rain forests are disappearing at an alarming rate. Annually losing vital habitats the size of Poland has profound consequences for the culturally diverse groups of indigenous peoples whose lives depend on these environments. Dependent upon the biological diversity of the forests, native people serve as the primary stewards

Figure 7.2 The dense vegetation of the Amazon rain forest near Manaus, Brazil, is seen in this photograph.

of their own ecosystems, so maintaining the region's cultural diversity is one of the first steps in the conservation of rain forest diversity.

Because the desire for fast income has fueled so much of the rain forest destruction, the goal now is to create economic incentives for indigenous people to protect and preserve the forests so as to yield long-term profits for themselves and their children. Currently, rain forests converted to cattle operations bring landowners approximately $60 an acre. Logging trees provides about $400 an acre. But when resources are harvested in a renewable manner, the land may yield as much as $2,000 per acre to the landowner.[14]

It is imperative, when harvesting from the rain forest, to employ and make use of the indigenous people and their knowledge. Native communities earn considerably more money carefully harvesting wild medicinal plants, fruits, nuts, and oils than they ever earned chopping down the forest to grow a few crops. Subsistence farming is a meager way of life. It is extremely difficult to continually grow crops or graze livestock on soil that was once a lush rain forest. When the rain forest is removed, its crucial soil-feeding and soil-building nutrients are lost along with that specific ecosystem.

In addition to the Amazon, other major rain forests of the world are found in Southeast Asia and Africa's Congo basin. In Southeast Asia lives a population of indigenous people known as the Orang Asli. As a group, the Orang Asli is divided into numerous tribes or subgroups depending on their way of life or their location. The diversity even among one group of natives creates a challenge for the ethnobotanists wishing to study plant use among a single group of people.

There is an urgency to create an inventory of useful plants native to this region. Ethnobotanists know that the Orang Asli are familiar with and utilize a large number of plants for food, medicine, and artifacts. However, there is not one complete inventory recorded for any of the various groups within this particular culture.

Food is of particular concern for Asia. Ethnobotanists believe that there are many species of food plants going unused in this region, even while Asia imports millions of dollars worth of food each year. A study of local food plants to determine which are best suited for sustainable farming, which provide the most nutrition, which are the most appealing, and which have the longest shelf-life may lead to Asia's local plants soon being able to compete profitably with the introduced foods currently on the market.

Like in so many other parts of the world where people still live so closely aligned to the natural world, the cultures of the African rain forests possess the ability to distinguish between edible and nonedible plants, poisonous or nonpoisonous plants, species with medicinal qualities, and even vegetation preferred by their livestock. Again, this knowledge is rarely written down. Instead, this essential information is passed from generation to generation, memorized by both parents and children alike.

Africa's rich diversity of languages and pastoral tribal systems both provide ethnobotanists with an important base of research. In contrast to many other rain forests where indigenous groups may not even have names for many of the plants they utilize, African tribes often have names for every organism they encounter. In addition, instead of being isolated, it is the tendency of many African tribes to travel—undoubtedly exchanging their knowledge with others around them.

The primary use of Africa's indigenous botanical knowledge is medicinal. The methods of preparing herbal remedies from plants are generally similar among Africans. In each preparation it is the healer's intention to withdraw whatever active properties are available from the plant before the plant's drug is provided to the patient. Whether that drug is administered in the form of a paste, a powder, or a liquid, or is inhaled, depends on the specific properties of the plant in question combined with the knowledge each healer possesses.

Boiling the roots and bark of trees or shrubs can create drug-infused teas that can be swallowed or bathed in, depending on the illness. Small leaves or tender plants are often crushed and then soaked in cold water before being swallowed. Sometimes leaves are burned and their ashes are rubbed onto wounds or soaked in water and gargled. For the treatment of stomach ailments, sore throats, or even venomous snakebite, specific plant leaves may be chewed and then swallowed in an effort to quickly release the potential benefits of the plant. If a poultice or bandage is required, succulent plant parts are often cooked or roasted to prepare them as part of a moist first aid dressing.

African healers are also unique in that they often create their own home gardens where the most important plants in their arsenal are grown and cultivated, eliminating the need to search the jungles for the essential plant in an emergency.

OF SPECIAL CONCERN

Perhaps the most pressing threats to rain forests can be found in three particular forests of the world; Brazil's Atlantic forest, the Choco' of South America's Pacific coast, and the African island of Madagascar (Figure 7.3).

The Atlantic forest was once considered one of the most densely rich ecosystems in the world, but now, sadly, almost all of the great rain forest has been destroyed, with perhaps less than 3 to 5% remaining.

As one of the wettest places on Earth, with an annual rainfall of over 30 feet (9.14 m) per year, the Choco' represents one of the least-collected regions in the world for ethnobotanists. Suffering from large clear-cutting, this piece of land lying along the Pacific Ocean is receiving a lot of attention in a race to stop the destruction and catalog the flora that remains.

Madagascar is considered by many botanists to be the number one conservation priority today. As much as 80% of the island's vegetation has been removed or disturbed during the past 1,000 years that people have lived on the island. The disappearance of this unique assemblage of plants affects the animal population

Figure 7.3 A Verreaux's sifaka, a type of lemur, feeds in a tree in southern Madagascar. It is named for its distinctive "si-fa-ka" call, which is used as a warning to other group members when predators are near.

as well. For a country so small, the numbers of native species found only on this tiny piece of Earth are startling; 40% of the island's birds, 90% of its primates, 98% of its frogs, and 100% of its rodents are found nowhere else.

Ironically, the destruction of the world's rain forests may represent the first time in history that plants have suffered from extinction on a large scale. Fossil evidence shows us that in the past, when organisms did fall to extinction, it was invariably the fauna, or animals, that suffered such a fate. In the case of the dinosaurs, it was inevitably a natural disaster or process of natural selection that brought about their demise. Human beings are responsible for the loss of the rain forests and the millions of organisms that depend on the rain forest ecosystems for life. If future sources of food and medicine elude us, we have only ourselves to blame.

8 Ethnobotany and Conservation

The care of the Earth is our most ancient and most worthy, and after all, our most pleasing responsibility. To cherish what remains of it, and to foster its renewal, is our only hope.

—Wendell Berry (1934–)
American novelist and poet

Ethnobotany and Conservation

The relationships between plants and people are profound, affecting nearly every aspect of our lives. Human cultures and plants, from prehistoric peoples and hunter-gatherers to our current world dominated by agriculture and industry, have always been woven together. What are the consequences of losing that plant diversity? What will happen as more and more rare or unknown species disappear because of human activities?

THE NAME IS NOT ENOUGH

In 1992, the Belize Association of Traditional Healers was formed as part of an effort to conserve species that are important to that country's complex work of traditional healers. The conservation effort emphasized the word *complex* when referring to the knowledge and cultural views possessed by indigenous people. Just knowing the name of a plant and preserving it is not enough. As ethnobotanists often repeat, the name alone will not heal you.

Most indigenous cultures perceive the Earth as sacred. This is an important distinction from Western tradition that values the Earth as a commodity: a source of food, building materials, medicine, beauty, and entertainment. Both views regard the natural environment as something worthy of protection. But it is the method of conservation and preservation that differs according to our values.

It is the worldview of the indigenous people, rather than the perception of developed countries, that the ethnobotanist seeks to conserve. Indigenous beliefs emphasize the need to protect the jungle, not because of its potential use to them, but because the jungle is a sacred place. The jungle's value is therefore intrinsic—valuable because it is there.

However, conserving places that loom large in our imaginations is a challenge. Jungles are still dark and mysterious places for many of us. European fables hide witches and warlocks in primitive forests. Dusty library books provide eyewitness accounts of headhunters and tiny men in the underbrush. Fairy tales tell of dragons returning to nest in the dark woods, clutching their latest victims in their talons. Children's bedtime stories often portray the most dangerous of beasts seeking shelter in the most inhospitable jungle. Jungles became destinations to be avoided at all costs—the place where orphaned children were raised by wolves, jaguars, or apes (Figure 8.1). As a matter of fact, the English word "savage" comes from the Latin word *sylvaticus,* meaning "of the woods." As a site of so much fear and wild imagination, it is no wonder that the need for conservation of our deepest rain forests was not fully appreciated until recently.

Fears and imaginations aside, forests have historically been cut down because they represent the simplest and quickest way to earn cash—by harvesting the timber, burning all that remains, and then planting a crop for a few seasons. Not surprisingly, this method of clear-cutting has serious implications for the environment. First, there is the immediate and devastating loss of the forest ecosystem and all the organisms living there. Second, there is the permanent loss of much of the region's nutrients. Most of the nutrients in a rain forest are found not in the soil, but in the tissues of the plants and animals living in that ecosystem. Ironically, whatever farming that follows faces the constant challenge of growing crops on poor soil in a location that once boasted some of the most fertile land on the planet. The large-scale removal of living ecosystems prevents rain forests from ever growing back. Perhaps most important, indigenous people have an incredible knowledge of the properties and uses of their local vegetation. Amassed over centuries, this knowledge is one of the first aspects of their culture to disappear when their ecosystems are disturbed.

THE ROLE OF INDIGENOUS PEOPLE IN CONSERVATION

A reconsideration of the role of indigenous people in conservation means understanding and accepting the view that the plants

Figure 8.1 An advertisement from 1921 for the movie *Adventures of Tarzan* shows Tarzan battling a lion, riding on an elephant, and fighting two men. Tarzan originally appeared in a novel by Edgar Rice Burroughs, in which the hero was orphaned as an infant and raised by apes.

can be sacred (Figure 8.2). Ethnobotanists believe that rain forest conservation will be best accomplished by adopting the views of indigenous people and acknowledging the contributions that indigenous knowledge of plants and resource management can make to Western culture.

Loss of **biodiversity** is the primary concern whenever natural resources are depleted. But we also need to consider loss of knowledge—the knowledge that only indigenous culture can provide about the uses of individual plants. It is the diversity of the natural ecosystems and the culture of the indigenous people living within them that must be protected together.

Figure 8.2 Children of Vanuata climb a fig tree. Vanuata is an archipelago of 83 islands in the South Pacific Ocean.

Until recently, indigenous people were seldom involved in the conservation of their own homes. Their opinion was rarely valued in the Western world, where most decisions about the use of the world's resources are made. And although developed nations, like the United States, Canada, Australia, New Zealand, Japan, and those in Western Europe, constitute only about 18% of the world's population, together they control almost 80% of the world's wealth.[15] Unfortunately, most of the world's endangered indigenous cultures and ecosystems are found in the undeveloped countries. The differences between the developed and the undeveloped nations (the "haves" and "have-nots" of the world) have often been at the root of conservation conflicts.

Western nations and indigenous people recognize the pressing need to protect vanishing species in their natural habitats and are trying to work together. Concerned about the loss of native plants used in weaving, the Maori of New Zealand organized a *hui,* or traditional conference inviting both scientists and traditional leaders to discuss strategies for conserving their native flora. Such collaboration is often complicated by cultural differences, but this effort was a success and the conference became an important model for future such collaborations. Most importantly, the conference demonstrated the three key positions advocated by indigenous peoples that recent ethnobotanical studies can prove with field evidence:

1. That all forest plants have a purpose and value

2. That the true economic, cultural, and spiritual values of rain forests and native habitats have scarcely been considered and are vastly underestimated

3. That entire cultures and ways of life will disappear if rain forests are destroyed

Is This a Model Plan for Rain Forest Communities?

In Peru there are communal reserves with specific rules concerning the removal of any natural resources. This proactive stance on the use of a region's products is a sign of progressive thinking. These rules are designed to help the local native community that benefits most from preserving their ecosystems—and stands to lose the most if those ecosystems are destroyed. After all, you preserve what you know best.

Here is a summary of a few of the rules as described in *Plants, People, and Culture—The Science of Ethnobotany*, by Michael J. Balick and Paul Alan Cox:

1. The extraction of forest timber is only permitted at the community level. It is prohibited for individuals, families, and groups to extract timber from the community reserve. Timber may only be removed when the community needs money for communal purposes, such as a new school or medicine for the village.

2. Fruits and medicinal plants may be removed by anyone who lives in that region. People from the community and from the neighboring communities can extract these products either for their own consumption or for the market.

3. Whenever collecting fruits, leaves, flowers, bark, resins, roots, and branches, all trees must be left standing. Special rules apply to the extraction of any particularly valuable species.

4. The community must decide as a group whether they will issue a permit to an outsider for the removal of any timber.

5. No farming is permitted in the area of the community forest reserve; however, the community recognizes the rights of its members over their old fallows for an unlimited time.

THE VALUES OF BIOLOGICAL DIVERSITY

Biological diversity is increasingly recognized for its importance beyond a purely scientific interest. The social and economic values of biodiversity are assuming greater significance as a range of different groups, including indigenous peoples, assert their claims and interests.

Conserving the world's ecosystems benefits all people. The reasons for conservation are many, but most would agree on at least the following:

1. Conserving ecosystems is an ethical issue. No species has the right to destroy another. Most societies, primitive and modern, promote a "live and let live" philosophy. Acknowledging that we share the world with many other species, we should not be responsible for the loss of any other species.

2. We conserve ecosystems for esthetic reasons. The beauty of all natural habitats should be protected.

3. We need to conserve our ecosystems for scientific reasons. Whether or not it is apparent to us now, any species may prove to have significant scientific value to the human population in the future. Protecting our environment now will help ensure the health and happiness of future generations.

4. We must conserve what is useful to us. We simply could not survive without the plants and animals on which our civilizations depend. Whether it is the plant-generated oxygen we breathe or domestic animals and crops that sustain enormous human populations, allowing any species to become endangered or extinct simply harms us in the end.

5. Perhaps the most urgent reason to conserve Earth's ecosystems is to retain the biodiversity of life. Biodiversity can be described as the variety of life on Earth. Ecosystems are complex and dynamic. They are living systems composed

of organisms constantly interacting with both living and nonliving components. Interaction is the key word here. The diversity found within any constantly changing ecosystem is what provides stability for the organisms living there.

Biodiversity also refers to the genetic diversity found within a species, such as the diversity of woodpeckers that live in the forest or the diversity of a desert ecosystem as opposed to the diversity of a forest ecosystem.

Earth's biodiversity is immense. Perhaps as many as 175 million species have been described, and many more than that exist on Earth today. Of all the groups of organisms we know of, the two groups that represent the highest amount of diversity are the insects, with almost one million different species, and the flowering plants, with at least 270,000 species.[16]

Because indigenous peoples possess knowledge of so many plants, ethnobotanists begin conservation there. That indigenous knowledge, however, is as endangered as some of the ecosystems. An inventory of medicinal plants compiled by the World Health Organization (WHO) in 1978 estimated that of 20,000 species known to benefit man, only 250 were used often enough to analyze and identify their main active chemical compounds. What is known is still mostly verbal and only partly documented within the history and folklore of native people.

Combine the loss of thousands of years of plant knowledge and use by indigenous people with the loss of the actual plants from deforestation, destruction of habitats, and alterations of ecosystems, and it's clear ethnobotanists have more work to do (Figure 8.3).

The slow assimilation of native culture into Western cultures is causing damage as well. The Yanomamo tribes of South America are rapidly losing their members to Western diseases. Native people often lack the natural immunity from diseases that people

A Look at Earth's Biodiversity

Species are the basic unit of biodiversity, but of the tens of millions of species that have existed on Earth, only a small percentage have been studied in detail. Amazingly, new species are still being discovered. Recently, the Nature Conservancy reported that a new species of honeyeater (a type of bird) was uncovered in New Guinea, and a furry lobster was found in the south Pacific. Even the ivory-billed woodpecker, thought to be extinct for decades, has recently had verifiable sightings in the swamps of the southeastern United States. Despite these discoveries, we know that other species are disappearing from Earth every day, even before they have been identified.

How many species exist on Earth? The Global Biodiversity Assessment, presented by the United Nations Environment Program in 1995, created a table of known and estimated species on Earth (Table 8.1). Though over a decade has passed since this latest working estimate, the numbers seem to remain the same due to the allowance in known species and working estimates.

Not all biologists agree with the United Nations estimates. But the total number of species still seems to fall within a staggering 1.45 million to 1.75 million. Some of the discrepancies are the result of the difficulties in classifying species. Obviously, classifying birds is not as challenging as classifying bacteria. While there are several thousand bird species living on Earth, one study found between 4,000 and 5,000 bacterial species in just one gram of soil!

To complicate matters, biodiversity is not evenly distributed among species—compare the small number of bear species found in the world to

from another culture may be incubating. Deadly outbreaks of smallpox nearly wiped out legions of North American Indians when the U.S. military forced them onto reservations a century ago. The Yanomamos of Brazil and Venezuela are suffering a similar fate. As the populations of these tribes dwindle, so goes the tens of thousands of beetle species known to exist. Also, biodiversity is not evenly distributed throughout the world. Seventy percent of the world's species are found in only 11 of the world's countries: Australia, Brazil, China, Colombia, Ecuador, India, Indonesia, Madagascar, Mexico, Peru, and Zaire. More than half of those species are found in the tropical rain forests.

Table 8.1   **Known and Estimated Species on Earth**

Taxonomic Group	# of Known Species	Working Estimated #s
Viruses	4,000	400,000
Bacteria	4,000	1,000,000
Fungi	72,000	1,500,000
Protozoa	40,000	200,000
Algae	40,000	400,000
Plants	270,000	320,000
Nematodes	25,000	400,000
Arthropods:		
Crustaceans	40,000	150,000
Arachnids	75,000	750,000
Insects	950,000	8,000,000
Mollusks	70,000	200,000
Chordates	45,000	50,000
Others	115,000	250,000
Total	1,750,000	13,620,000

their art and culture. Their knowledge is rarely if ever recorded in written form and therefore is not protected.

Organizations like Hands Around the World focus on preserving the culture of these people by encouraging the continuation of their native art forms. The goal is not only to preserve the

Figure 8.3 Ethnobotanists search for wild pepper specimens near a Toba tribal settlement in Paraguay.

art itself but also their culture by giving them a viable means of support using their traditional skills. Too often, native people—especially in the Amazon rain forest—are forced to embark in nontraditional and ecologically harmful methods of supporting their families like the "slash and burn" farming that destroys the rain forest in exchange for quick access to money. By encouraging and supporting traditional art forms, groups like Hands Around the World help preserve native cultures, their way of life, and most importantly, the natural ecosystems those cultures depend on. Losing just one tribe, just one small portion of the Yanomamo culture, represents an important loss of diversity to the regions.

Preserving genetic diversity is as crucial as preserving biodiversity. Gene cells from wild species of plants are being preserved now in order to later strengthen the gene pool of an endangered species, if necessary. A diverse gene pool can save plants from succumbing to disease. This is especially useful in agriculture where we often rely on only one plant crop and grow that crop in enormous quantities. Take, for example, barley. The common crop has a narrow genetic base leading to a greater vulnerability to disease and pests. In the past century only about 20 varieties of barley have made up the majority of North America's barley crop. This concerns growers and breeders because of recent warning signs: since 1994, two blights that targeted barley have caused billion-dollar losses to farmers.

The conservation of biodiversity protects the genetic base found in each plant species, maintaining their adaptability and biological health. The conservation of indigenous people and their indigenous knowledge is important historically and culturally as the relationships indigenous people share with their environments reflect our own past relationships with the natural world.

Notes

1. John Harshberger, "What Is Ethnobotany and Why Is It Important?," Ethnobotany at Fort Lewis College. Available online at http://anthro.fortlewis.edu/ethnobotany/ethno2.htm

2. Patricia Barnes-Svarney, "The Plant Kingdom," *The New York Public Library Science Desk Reference.* New York: Simon & Schuster Macmillan Company, 1995, p. 104.

3. Bonnie Okonek, "Introduction: What's in a Name," Classification of Plants. Available online at http://www.accessexcellence.org/RC/Ethnobotany/page3.html

4. Richard Law, "The Emergence of Sedentary Agriculture," Agricultural Revolution – Emergence of Agriculture. Available online at http://www.wsuedu/gened/learn-modules/top_agrev//4-Agriculture/agriculture2.html

5. "Quinoa" Whole Health MD. Available online at http://www.wholehealthmd.com/refshelf/foods_view/0,1523,74,00.html

6. Michael J. Balick and Paul Alan Cox, *Plants, People, and Culture: The Science of Ethnobotany.* New York: Scientific American Library, 1996, p. 117.

7. Ibid.

8. David W. Tschanz, "Herbal Contraception in Ancient Times," Islam Online.net, 2003. Available online at http://www.islam-oline.net/English/Science/2003/08/article02.shtml

9. Balick and Cox. p. 25.

10. Ibid., p. 176.

11. Ibid., p. 161.

12. Rain Forest Web, "Indigenous Peoples," Rainforestweb.org. Available online at http://www.rainforestweb.org/Rainforest_Information/Indigenous_Peoples/

13. Leslie Taylor, "The Disappearing Rain Forests," Rainforest Facts. 2004. Available online at http://www.raintree-health.co.uk/data/rainforestfacts1.html

14. Ibid.

15. Richard T. Wright, *Environmental Science*, 9th ed. Saddle River, NJ: Pearson Education, 2005, p. 127.

16. Ibid., p. 275.

Agriculture The business or science of cultivating the soil, growing crops, and raising livestock.

Alkaloid Physically active, nitrogen-containing organic bases obtained from plants, including nicotine, quinine, cocaine, and morphine.

Assimilate To absorb an immigrant or culturally distinct group into another culture.

Biodiversity The diversity of living things found in the natural world. The concept usually refers to different species but also includes ecosystems and the genetic diversity within a given species.

Botany The study of plants.

Canopy The layer formed by the upper branches of trees in a forest.

Chicle The milky juice of a tropical plant used in chewing gum.

Code of Hammurabi The first written code of law in human history, dated about 1770 B.C.

Compounds A combination of two or more elements.

Conquistadors Spanish conquerors of Mexico and Peru.

Curare Resinous extracts of variable chemical composition, obtained from several species of South American trees of the genera *Chondrodendron* and *Strychnos*.

Dicotyledons Plants characterized by embryonic seed leaves that appear at germination.

Ecosystem A grouping of plants, animals, and other organisms interacting with each other and with their environment in a sustainable manner.

Ethnobotany The study of how cultures make use of the plants in their ecosystems.

Food and Drug Administration (FDA) A government agency responsible for advancing public health by assuring the safety of human and veterinary drugs, biological products, and medical devices.

Genetic diversity The diversity of genes found in various breeds, species, varieties, etc., of organisms.

Genus Classification of a group of similar organisms; a genus consists of one or more species.

Glossary

Hallucinogens Plant-based drugs that induce hallucinations for recreational or religious purposes.

Indigenous Living or occurring naturally in a specific area or environment.

Monocotyledons One of the two major divisions of angiosperms, marked by a single embryonic seed leaf at germination.

Monoculture The practice of growing the same crop year after year on the same land, as opposed to crop rotation.

Neanderthal An extinct race of human ancestors that lived during the late Pleistocene epoch and is associated with Paleolithic tools.

Nomad A member of a group of people who wander from place to place.

Pharaoh A king of ancient Egypt.

Photosynthesis The chemical process carried on by green plants through which light energy is used to produce glucose from carbon dioxide and water. Oxygen is released as a by-product.

Polymers Any of numerous natural and synthetic compounds.

Poultice An herbal paste made by mashing plant materials with a liquid.

Quinine A crystal alkaloid obtained from cinchona and used as a drug to fight malaria and other diseases.

Shaman A priest of an indigenous culture who is believed to summon spirits.

Species A group of closely related organisms that are capable of interbreeding.

Sustainable The process of continuing indefinitely without depleting the energy or material resources on which you depend.

Subsistence Meeting the food needs of farmers and their families, with little else earned. A practice of farming seen most often in developing countries.

Taxonomy The science of identifying and classifying organisms according to their natural relationships.

Vascular The conductive tissue of plants, which absorb water and nutrients through their roots and circulate that fluid throughout the plant.

Balick, Michael J, and Paul Alan Cox. *Plants, People, and Culture: The Science of Ethnobotany.* New York: Scientific American Library, 1996.

Barnes-Svarney, Patricia. *The New York Public Library Science Desk Reference.* New York: The Stonesong Press, Inc. and the New York Public Library, 1995.

Beazley, John D. *The Way Nature Works.* New York: Macmillan General Reference, 1992.

Berlin, Brent. *Ethnobiological Classification—Principles of Categorization of Plants and Animals in Traditional Societies.* Princeton, NJ: Princeton University Press, 1992.

Caduto, Michael J., and Joseph Bruchac. *Keepers of the Earth: Native American Stories and Environmental Activities for Children.* Golden, CO: Fulcrum Publishing Company, 1998.

Caufield, Catherine. *In the Rainforest: Report from a Strange, Beautiful, Imperiled World.* Chicago: University of Chicago Press, 1985.

Chagnon, N. *Yanomamo: The Last Days of Eden.* New York: Harcourt, Brace Jovanovich, 1992.

Christman, Carolyn J., D. Phillip Sponenberg, and Donald E. Bixby. *A Rare Breeds Album of American Livestock.* Pittsboro, NC: American Livestock Breeds Conservancy, 1997.

Davis, Wade. *One River: Explorations and Discoveries in the Amazon Rain Forest.* New York: Simon & Schuster, 1996.

Diamond, Jared. *Guns, Germs, and Steel: The Fates of Human Societies.* New York: W. W. Norton & Company, 1999.

Fargis, Paul. *The New York Public Library Desk Reference, 4th ed.,* New York: Hyperion, 2002.

Gunderson, Mary, and Dennis Dahlin. *The Food Journal of Lewis & Clark: Recipes for an Expedition.* Yankton, SD: History Cooks, 2003.

Harshberger, Dr. John. "What Is Ethnobotany and Why Is It Important?" Ethnobotany at Fort Lewis College. Available online at http://anthro.fortlewis.edu/ethnobotany/ethno2.htm

Heckewelder, Rev. John. *History, Manners, and Customs of The Indian Nations Who Once Inhabited Pennsylvania and the Neighboring States.* Philadelphia: Publication Fund of the Historical Society of Pennsylvania, 1876. Facsimile reprint: Bowie, MD: Heritage Books, 1990.

Heywood, V. H., ed. *Global Biodiversity Assessment.* New York: Cambridge University Press, 1995.

Bibliography

Kent, Barry C. *Susquehanna's Indians*. Harrisburg, PA: Commonwealth of Pennsylvania, The Pennsylvania Historical and Museum Commission, 1984.

Moerman, Daniel. *Native American Ethnobotany*. Portland, Or: Timber Press, 1998.

Okonek, Bonnie. "Introduction: What's in a Name." Classification of Plants. Available online at http://www.accessexcellence.org/RC/Ethnobotany/page3.html

Plotkin, Mark J., PH.D. *Tales of a Shaman's Apprentice—An Ethnobotanist Searches for New Medicines in the Amazon Rain Forest*. New York: Viking Penguin, 1993.

Rain Forest Web. "Indigenous Peoples," Rainforestweb.org, 2006. Avaialble online at http://www.rainforestweb.org/Rainforest_Information/Indigenous_Peoples/

Raintree Health. "The Disappearing Rainforests," Rainforest Facts, 2004. Available online at http://www.raintree-health.co.uk/data/rainforestfacts1.html

Reidel, Jon. "Bioprospecting in Madagascar," The View/From the University of Vermont, 2004. Available online at http://www.uvm.edu/theview/article.php?id=1438

Renfrew, Jane M. *Palaeoethnobotany: The Prehistoric Food Plants of the Near East and Europe*. New Haven, CT: Columbia University Press, 1973.

Rountree, Helen C., and Thomas E. Davidson. *Eastern Shore Indians of Virginia and Maryland*. Charlottesville, VA: University of Virginia Press, 1998.

Schultes, Richard Evans, and Siri von Reis. *Ethnobotany: Evolution of a Discipline*. Portland, OR: Dioscorides Press, 1995.

Schultes, Richard Evans, Albert Hofmann. *Plants of the Gods*. Rochester, VT: Inner Traditions International, 1992.

Taylor, Leslie. "The Disappearing Rain Forests," Rainforest Facts, 2004. Available online at http://www.raintree-health.co.uk/data/rainforest-facts1.html

Viola, Herman J. and Carolyn Margolis. *Seeds of Change: A Quincentennial Commemoration*. Washington, DC: Smithsonian Books, 1991.

Waak, Patricia, and Kenneth Strom. *Sharing the Earth: Cross-Cultural Experiences in Population, Wildlife and the Environment*. New York: The National Audubon Society, 1992.

Wright, Richard T. *Environmental Science, 9th ed.* Saddle River, NJ: Pearson Education, Inc., 2005.

Balick, Michael J, and Paul Alan Cox. *Plants, People, and Culture, The Science of Ethnobotany.* New York: Scientific American Library, 1996.

Beazley, John D. *The Way Nature Works.* New York: Macmillan General Reference, 1992.

Caduto, Michael J., and Joseph Bruchac. *Keepers of the Earth: Native American Stories and Environmental Activities for Children.* Golden, CO: Fulcrum Publishing Company, 1998.

Caufield, Catherine. *In the Rainforest: Report from a Strange, Beautiful, Imperiled World.* Chicago, IL: University of Chicago Press, 1985.

Christman, Carolyn J., D. Phillip Sponenberg, and Donald E. Bixby. *A Rare Breeds Album of American Livestock.* Pittsboro, NC: American Livestock Breeds Conservancy, 1997.

Gunderson, Mary, and Dennis Dahlin. *The Food Journal of Lewis & Clark: Recipes for an Expedition.* Yankton, SD: History Cooks, 2003.

Viola, Herman J. and Carolyn Margolis. *Seeds of Change: A Quincentennial Commemoration.* Washington, DC: Smithsonian Books, 1991.

Waak, Patricia, and Kenneth Strom. *Sharing the Earth: Cross-Cultural Experiences in Population, Wildlife and the Environment.* New York: The National Audubon Society, 1992.

Web Sites

An Introduction to Ethnobotany
A comprehensive introduction to this field.
www.accessexcellence.org/RC/Ethnobotany/

Aromatic and Medicinal Plants Index
An archive of plants (with photographs and detailed information).
www.hort.purdue.edu/newcrop/med-aro/toc.html

Center for World Indigenous Studies
A site to promote the ideas and knowledge of indigenous peoples.
www.cwis.org

Conservation International
Protecting Earth's biodiversity around the world.
www.conservation.org

Green Machine: PCA Medicinal Plant Working Group's Website
Informative Web site maintained by the Plant Conservation Alliance.
www.nps.gov/plants/medicinal/

Further Reading

Indigenous Peoples Survival Foundation
A nonprofit whose mission is to promote understanding between ancient traditional cultures and modern civilization.
www.indigenouspeople.org

IUCN—The World Conservation Union
The world's largest conservation organization, encompassing 138 countries.
www.iucn.org

Medicinal Plants List
A site listing the most common medicinal plants in use today.
www.world.std.com/~krahe/html1.html

NativeWeb
Resources for indigenous cultures around the world.
www.nativeweb.org

Rainforest Alliance
An alliance that protects rain forests through changes in land use.
www.rainforest-alliance.org

The Rainforest Site
Interactive site explaining how you can preserve a piece of the rain forest.
www.therainforestsite.com

Tropical American Tree Farms
Information on how farmers are growing tropical trees in a sustainable manner.
http://tropicaltreefarms.com

Wildlife Conservation Society
Managing national and international conservation projects.
www.wcs.org

Index

Index

page:

About the Author

Kim J. Young received her B.S. degree from Wilmington College in Ohio, where she studied biology and environmental science. She received her M.A. in science writing from Johns Hopkins University in Baltimore, Maryland. She lives in York county, Pennsylvania, where she works for the local conservation district, teaches as an adjunct faculty member, and writes about topics focusing on the preservation of rural traditions.